What people are saying about …

WHEN GOD BREAKS YOUR HEART

"Every sufferer looks longingly to Christ and secretly asks, *How could you let this happen?* My friend Ed Underwood asked that question openly from his deathbed. We all knew that Ed's only hope was Christ's answer to our plea. Jesus answered, and Ed lives and serves. This is his story—a story I highly recommend, a story that will show you how to take Christ's hand through your darkest days."

Bruce Wilkinson, speaker and author of the #1 New York Times best seller *The Prayer of Jabez*

"Ed enters into the fellowship of suffering by letting us know he's got the credentials. This is not a book written by an outsider to pain. It is not a collection of helpful hints from someone who doesn't understand. That's what makes me listen to what he has to say. In a skillful way he enters into my own room of pain, makes me feel comfortable that he is 'one of us,' and gently leads me in the direction that I so desperately want and need but which my pain and anger have made it repulsive to go."

Rich Buhler, founder of TruthOrFiction.com, broadcast journalist, speaker, and best-selling author

"What a joy to know that brokenness, when it happens, is not the endgame of life. Jesus lived His life to repair the broken and to restore the wounded. If you believe that the psalmist was right when he said, 'God is close to the brokenhearted and saves those who are crushed in spirit' (Ps. 34:18), then this book will lead you to an experience of that promise!"

Dr. Joseph M. Stowell III, president of Cornerstone University, speaker, and author of *The Trouble with Jesus, Following Christ, Simply Jesus and You*, and *Radical Reliance*

"This book is life changing. Its down-to-earth approach in dealing with those 'why God' moments is refreshing and relevant to anyone who has had problems—or should I say, anyone who is breathing. I found myself laughing, crying, relating, and questioning with Ed. By the end of this book you feel as if you and Ed are the best of friends, because of the emotional honesty and vulnerability that he invested into this book."

Sarah Kelly, Grammy-nominated Gotee recording artist

"Why do we allow discouragement to take active root in our hearts? For me, the best way to turn darkness into light is by reflecting on the experiences of those who've been called upon to carry incredibly heavy burdens. That's why the life journey of Ed Underwood so resonates with my spirit. What you'll especially appreciate is Ed's complete openness and vulnerability. He virtually allows you to walk in his shoes along a treacherous journey none of us would ordinarily choose for ourselves. Your life won't be the same after you experience the blessing that uniquely comes *When God Breaks Your Heart.*"

Al Sanders, founder of Ambassador Advertising Agency

“I’ve known and respected Ed Underwood for years. He’s an honest and godly man, and this is a transparent and powerful book. If you doubt God’s love or you know someone who’s hurting, this is the book to read.”

Dr. Donald R. Sunukjian, professor of preaching, Talbot School of Theology and author of *Invitation to Biblical Preaching*

“I have known Ed Underwood for over two decades. He has always been a man of integrity and passion. But something happened when God broke Ed’s heart. He emerged stronger, more appreciative, and more fully alive. Ed now lives to serve and he is doing that well. His story of near death and chronic illness is raw, honest, and real. You will be encouraged that you can face adversity and discover that God is faithful. I am blessed to be his friend.”

Dave Burchett, author of *When Bad Christians Happen to Good People* and contributor to *Crosswalk.com*

“Because Ed is my dear friend, the story of his broken heart breaks my heart. But Ed’s painful journey also deeply encourages me that the same Jesus who met Mary and Martha at the tomb of their brother Lazarus, the same Jesus who met Ed in his bloated, frightened, tormented, itching, T-cell carcinoma despair ... **that same Jesus** will meet me and those I serve in our suffering. Thank you, Ed, for allowing your broken heart to teach us that Jesus cares about our broken hearts, that He will come when we call and that in the long run, our suffering will display the very glory of God!”

J. Kevin Butcher, pastor of Hope Community Church of Detroit

"You will never read the story of Lazarus in the same way again. Through his own heart-wrenching suffering, Ed Underwood insightfully teaches us how to trust God before the pain has passed—the same lessons Jesus intended for Mary and Martha to learn. If you experience these truths, hope will pervade your life."

Dr. Bruce McNicol and **Bill Thrall,** coauthors of the bestselling *TrueFaced* and *The Ascent of a Leader,* founders of Leadership Catalyst

"When tragedy strikes repeatedly, it's more than most of us can bear. Yet out of the most devastating life experiences, the Lord longs to craft within us a new, stronger, more vibrant and enduring faith. He wants to do the same as you read Ed Underwood's powerful, utterly honest, and deeply moving book."

David Sanford, author of *If God Disappears*

"The university I work at is in the shadow of Pastor Ed Underwood's ministry, just down the road from his church. Many of our community members attend and speak highly of his shepherds' heart and pastor's wisdom. I have also found him to be both transparent and passionate about God's work in his own life even in tremendously difficult challenges. After reading *When God Breaks Your Heart,* I can now add to this description of him that of inspiring, powerful, and transformational author! Through the story of the death and resurrection of Lazarus, Ed gently shows the compassion, grace, and love Jesus has for all of us. This remarkable work birthed out of Ed's unspeakable pain and suffering brought the pieces of God's truth together for me and will for anyone else trying to find God in the midst of the unthinkable."

Jon Wallace, president of Azusa Pacific University

"Ed Underwood's raw honesty in *When God Breaks Your Heart* is as refreshing as it is poignant. He takes the reader on his journey through deep human pain and the darker places of the night with transparent conversations with God. This book does not fall back on trite platitudes for answers but grapples with the nature of God and profound biblical insights to point others to the hope in Christ that Ed found through his own odyssey. For me, knowing the depth of the man makes the depth of the book even more compelling."

Barry Corey, president of Biola University

When God Breaks Your Heart

Choosing Hope in the Midst of Faith-Shattering Circumstances

ED UNDERWOOD

Foreword by Joni Eareckson Tada

WHEN GOD BREAKS YOUR HEART
Published by David C. Cook
4050 Lee Vance View
Colorado Springs, CO 80918 U.S.A.

David C. Cook Distribution Canada
55 Woodslee Avenue, Paris, Ontario, Canada N3L 3E5

David C. Cook U.K., Kingsway Communications
Eastbourne, East Sussex BN23 6NT, England

LCCN: 2008931896
ISBN 978-1-4347-6751-6

Published in association with the literary agency of D. C. Jacobson & Associates LLC, an Author Management Company.
www.dcjacobson.com

The Team: Don Pape, Gudmund Lee, Amy Kiechlin,
Jaci Schneider, and Susan Vannaman
Cover Design: BMB Design, Scott Johnson
Interior Design: The DESK, Katherine Lloyd
Cover Photo: © iStock
Author Photo: Shannon Mocabee

Printed in the United States of America
First Edition 2008

2 3 4 5 6 7 8 9 10

052709

For all who—like Mary and Martha—look at the tragedy in their lives and wonder why Jesus doesn't show up … but still look for Him with broken hearts …

and

To my life-partner, Judy, and our children, who never gave up on God, even when I did

CONTENTS

ACKNOWLEDGMENTS

Without my wife, Judy, my faith would have faltered. Without her prayer, I would have died. Without her encouragement, I would never have written this book.

Judy, my family, and I wish to thank all who kneel with us at the throne of grace, begging God to let me live and serve—especially our truly healing community, Church of the Open Door.

I'm especially grateful to Bruce Wilkinson, who told me that I should write this book; to Al Sanders and Joni Eareckson Tada, who told me I could write this book; and to Don Jacobson, who told me I would write this book. My thanks to Jenni Burke and the team at D. C. Jacobson & Associates, and also to Don Pape, Gudmund Lee, and the team at David C. Cook.

BEFORE YOU BEGIN ...

God extends His hand and offers you life abundant and joy unspeakable, for here and eternity. But do you ever wonder how much it could cost? The answer is short, simple, and painful. "It will cost you *everything*," God replies.

It's not the answer most of us expect. It's not what the rich young ruler expected when he asked Jesus how he could have eternal life. Jesus told the young man to go out and sell everything he had, give the money to the poor, and follow Him as Lord. The young man could not bear the cost. And so he walked away the loser.

Most of us trifle with the cost of Christianity. We slap our sins on the table and, for the price of Somebody Else's blood, happily walk away with an asbestos-lined soul and a title deed to heaven. With "eternity" taken care of, we get back to living life as usual, offering the obligatory gestures to God on Sundays and holidays.

But God doesn't let us get away with that. Jesus said, "Anyone who does not take his cross and follow me is not worthy of me. Whoever finds his life will lose it, and whoever loses his life for my sake will find it" (Matt. 10:38–39 NIV). What was true for the rich young ruler is true for us. God is constantly reminding us of what it costs to be a follower of Christ. And it hurts.

It's why my heart resonates with Ed Underwood's. He knows the cost. He knows that God always seems to be pointing to one more area of our life that needs to come under His domain. "Ouch!" Suffering *hurts*. Especially the kind of suffering Ed has experienced these many years. But this gentle man has learned that God will persevere at whatever point we resist. So every day Ed loses his life for Christ's sake and, in so doing, finds life abundant and joy unspeakable.

Pastor Ed's insights and wisdom are not espoused from a pulpit elevated above my experience. He doesn't package truth in platitudes. He doesn't speak about suffering—or about God—in trivial tones. Rather, he shares hard-fought-for wisdom that's been sifted through suffering, like grain gleaned from a thresher.

After more than forty years of quadriplegia, I'm *still* learning the cost of following my Savior. But it's becoming clearer. I see that pain is a bruising of a blessing; but a blessing, nonetheless. It's a strange, dark companion; but still, a companion. It drives me deeper into the fellowship of sharing in Christ's afflictions, and closer to that place of intimacy with Jesus that is sweeter than words can describe. As someone once wrote, I receive pain as from the left hand of God. Yet the left one is better than no hand at all. *Much* better.

It's the way Ed Underwood looks at things too. I'm convinced that as you read this highly personal and transparent book, you will discover the blessed cost of following the Savior as well. Why else would you pick up a book titled *When God Breaks Your Heart* … unless you've been there, unless you've experienced the pain and you want to know what's beyond the heartbreak. Well, the horizon is bright and beautiful. More beautiful than anything you could imagine. So welcome to the club. Welcome to the pages of this exceptional book. Welcome to what it *truly* means to follow God.

—Joni Eareckson Tada
Joni and Friends International Disability Center
Winter 2008

We pray that you'll have the strength to stick it out over the long haul—not the grim strength of gritting your teeth but the glory-strength God gives. It is strength that endures the unendurable and spills over into joy, thanking the Father who makes us strong enough to take part in everything bright and beautiful that he has for us.

—Colossians 1:11–12 MSG

PREFACE

Ever wonder how God could watch what is happening to you or someone you love and not intervene? If you haven't, you will. And knowing that God could do something about it will break your heart.

This is a book to help you or someone you love through the darkest days and nights. It's about people who have found a way to cling to God when others have walked away. There is little here for the philosopher or the theologian looking for a fresh approach to the "problem of suffering." There is much here for those whose problem *is* suffering.

In the pages ahead you'll find the freedom to admit what everyone feels when life hurts more than is imaginable—*God has let me down.* I know. I live with a chronic leukemia that viciously attacks my skin with disfiguring and debilitating pain. As a dedicated Christian, my heart was broken to think that God didn't care for me enough to remove this deadly disease from my life.

When I decided it wasn't worth it to follow Jesus anymore, the story of Lazarus's family changed my mind. Jesus' tender care for Martha and Mary convinced me that I was still His personal concern. In this familiar story from the gospel of John, I found the strength and hope I needed to live life from this aging and broken vessel.

As you read the story of this family that was closer to Jesus than any other, you might think John had your particular pain in mind when he wrote it. You will ask for Jesus' care openly and feel His love in the ones He sends to your side. Most of all, you will see in His promises to Martha and Mary the keys to releasing *all* the good He intended to come from your private tragedy. What you'll discover will open your life to His unique place of blessing because of your circumstances. And you'll begin to live with unshakable hope that His love is guiding you along the path of life.

After discovering your path of blessing through *their* story, you will learn more about what it takes to walk that path through *my* story. In part 2, I want to walk you through some of the most difficult thresholds our suffering brings—by telling you some of the ways I experienced it firsthand, and how I dealt with it.

You might be surprised to know that you are not alone in your doubts and that you're set free to express your true feelings to God. You will be comforted to know that Jesus' heart is breaking with yours. And when you discover how to experience His most intimate care, you will know why your suffering means that your greatest impact and influence for God is in front of you. I pray you will take God's hand and mine, as we walk forward in hope together.

—Ed Underwood
Pastor, Church of the Open Door
Glendora, California

Part I

When God Breaks Your Heart

Chapter 1

IF YOU HAD BEEN HERE

My personal crisis of suffering happened the night I almost lost my grip on faith in a sweat-soaked, blood-stained bed. My daughter's family had just returned from a day trip to Disneyland and wanted to spend some time at Papa and Boppie's home in the foothills north of Los Angeles. But Judy, my wife (Boppie to the grandchildren), and I were feeling less and less like the grandparents we used to be. Our life as we had known it was slipping away. I was very, very sick.

As the three grandkids bounced in with stories of pirates and princesses, I retreated upstairs. Judy followed me to our bedroom, which had become our secret place to cry together and beg God for mercy. *How long will You ignore our anguish? What do You want from us? Have we failed You in some way? Why won't You give us our life back?*

I lay in our bed trying not to think about the torment of another night in this condition. "Come on, honey, let's pray," Judy whispered through her tears. "You'll need to be quieter tonight when you pray. I know your heart is broken and I can't imagine your misery, but your wailing will upset the babies."

"Don't worry, sweetie," I answered coldly. "I'm through praying, tonight or any night. You pray if you want, but I'm not talking to God any more."

With a few decades as a pastor under my belt, I had heard many Christians claim they were through with prayer. I never believed they meant it. Now I do. I meant it that night. With all my heart I meant it.

I have had many close-up encounters with suffering, both physical and emotional. My years as a firefighter and soldier left a body scarred from injuries and surgeries. I have cried and prayed with friends through the worst life has to offer. Personal regrets have kept me on repentant knees through many sleepless nights.

Through all of this, I had never fully understood believers who give up on God ... until this night the malaise of my disease—Sezary syndrome—made it perfectly clear: Even those of us with hearts wholly given to God will give up on Him when we feel He has given up on us.

EVEN THOSE OF US WITH HEARTS WHOLLY GIVEN TO GOD WILL GIVE UP ON HIM WHEN WE FEEL HE HAS GIVEN UP ON US.

If you read about my disease in a medical journal, you would discover that it is a "late and ominous development of cutaneous T-cell lymphoma" that "likely represents the luekemic phase." And that the "typical patient is an adult with generalized erythoderma, pururitis (itching)" in danger of progressing to "extensive organ involvement."

What you won't read are the gory details that only victims writing on blogs and sitting in cancer waiting rooms will share. As our skin falls off and the blood and body fluids seep through whatever bloody wrap we choose for that day, the infernal itching drives us to scar our own tissue as we scratch and dig in a desperate attempt to soothe the pain—until many just give up and die. Or worse, swallow one of the many bottles of pills our oncologists give us to try to ease our suffering.

Rather than give up on life and choose suicide, I chose to lose hope and give up on God.

When I expressed my crisis of faith to Judy, she knew I had crossed over a dangerous line of doubt to a cynical and treacherous place. With our years of experience in ministry, we both knew I might never return to her side as a disciple of the Savior.

Shaken by my disbelief, Judy rebuked me in tears. "Honey, you don't mean this. The Lord is all we have, all we have ever had. He is our life. Don't say this, please. This is just the medicine talking. I can't imagine your pain and distress, but you can't give up on God!"

"Yes, I can," I said. "I just did."

"How? How do you just throw away our life in a moment? It doesn't make sense!"

"Yes, it does," I explained with effortless logic and indifference. "He's supposed to be my heavenly Father, right?"

"You know He is," she said quietly.

"And He claims to be a loving and compassionate Father who cares for His children, right?"

I knew I'd hit a nerve when Judy didn't object to that sentence.

"I'm a father myself and I know a father's heart," I said. "I would not let this happen to my child if there was any way I could prevent it. *Not my child*. If He truly cares for His children, I'm not one of them."

Her silence betrayed her weakening resistance to my reasoning. I had a point. This brutal disease had reduced her husband to a cruel caricature of his former self. But to my eternal blessing, Judy held to her faith even as mine was collapsing.

PLEASE BRING HIM BACK!

"I'm not going to argue with you about this," Judy told me. "I choose to trust God and ask Him to bring you back to both of us—Him *and* me."

The answer to her prayer came from one of the most familiar stories in the Bible. I had always considered this to be the story about a man named Lazarus, a man the Lord Jesus miraculously raised from the dead. Now I see it as the story of his sisters' faith.

As my evening medications mercifully eased the pain and subdued the insufferable itching, my mind cleared somewhat. The scenes of John 11 played over and over as I battled to stay true to my vain resolve not to think about Jesus. I could not ignore the protests of Martha and Mary. Unrehearsed, each rushed to Jesus with the exact same brokenhearted complaint: "Lord, if You had been here, my brother would not have died" (John 11:21, 32).

That was my line, my grievance: *Lord, You could have prevented this! I would never let this happen to anyone I loved, especially not my child. How can You tell me my Father in heaven loves me as*

His child? I'm not His child; if I were, You would have shown up sooner. You wouldn't have broken my heart!

I fell asleep drawn irresistibly to the experience of these two desperately disappointed women who had walked with my Savior.

Alone the next day, I retrieved my Bible from the corner I had tossed it to in anger. I turned to John 11. Maybe there was something here for me. Wrapped in the blood-spattered quilt that regulated my body's temperature in the absence of skin, I read verses 1–44 as if for the first time. Poring over the Lord's words to His followers again and again, I begged Him for the hope my heart needed to go on.

I found it that day in John's eyewitness account of the words and tears of Jesus. Some things I had never seen before—because I had never hurt beyond hope—suddenly opened my eyes and my heart to the love of my Savior.

When Judy returned home from work later that day, I shared these insights with her. We knew that God had used these truths to answer her prayer—He had brought me back to her … and to Him.

I knew I was still His child.

Before You Give Up on God

If your physical or emotional turmoil is stealing your confidence in God, I want to share these comforting truths about Jesus' love and care for you and give you every assurance that you are God's child. As Jesus' words penetrate your heart, you will begin to think differently about your pain and find the strength to continue. More than that, *you will begin to actually live expectantly again*, certain of God's direction and influence in your life.

Years after that night of suffering, still living with this chronic and deadly disease, I remain sure. And so do many others I have met around the world. Regardless of the topic of the sermon or seminar, the desperate and disappointed always find me. Some are ashamed of the same doubts and questions I voiced that night, when I, like them, felt I was losing my faith.

"I have to tell you, Ed, if you can't give me a reason to reconsider, I'm through with God," one honest pastor told me. "You said you were ready to give up on prayer. That's exactly where I am right now. Why should I cry out to Jesus? He never shows up!"

"Lord, if You had been here ..."

Over dinner in a hospitality house for career Christian workers in Central Africa, a despairing woman who had served Christ for years on the frontier of faith said to me, "Ed, I am ready to suffer and serve for the rest of my life. But my sister's twin daughters back home are dying ... again. Thousands of committed Christians around the world have been praying for my nieces for years. But their suffering continues. Why won't God either take these babies or heal them? I've always been told He doesn't trifle with us. Now I don't know. Why doesn't He step in? I mean, they're just children."

"Lord, if You had been here ..."

"Why do I have hepatitis when I have lived a life free of drugs and illicit sex? If I'm His child, then why didn't He give this disease to someone who doesn't belong to Him and who deserves it?"

"Lord, if You had been here ..."

"All I ever wanted was a Christian home. We met in Bible

school! Why did God bring this unfaithful man into my life? Why do I have to raise my children alone while all these women who couldn't care less seem to have it so easy?"

"Lord, if You had been here ..."

"Look at all the children living in homes where there is no love, no care, even rejection and abuse. We have begged God for a child, but the doctors tell us we will never have a baby. Why does our home have to be childless?"

"Lord, if You had been here ..."

My answer is always the same: "All I can say is that when I felt just like you're feeling right now, the story of Martha and Mary at their brother's grave dramatically transformed my life."

In hundreds of conversations, without exception, the principles from John 11 bring what I can only call a "grace revival" to every believing heart.

Since you haven't put this book down, you're probably looking for a grace revival of your own. You wonder if Jesus' words to His followers that day offer any hope to you. You keep your dark secret—that you wonder if He is still in your life—even as you beg Him for evidence. When you pray, you find it hard to admit to the One you have always thought of as powerful and good that you feel betrayed.

You might be wondering what you would—or *should*—say to God in light of your circumstances. To be honest, I wondered the same thing. In the next chapter you will discover what I believe God taught me about prayer through the story of Mary and Martha. But right now, let me simply encourage you to give prayer another try.

Dear fellow sufferer, God knows your turmoil. He is aware of your words before they leave your tongue. Your secret feelings today were known to Him before you were born. He is neither surprised nor threatened by your doubts and fears. I believe that His mighty hand has brought you to this book, this paragraph, and this very sentence. His love has not let you go, but has prepared you for the lessons of faith His followers learned centuries ago in the village of Bethany.

If you can find it in your heart to come to Him one more time, may I suggest a prayer?

This is a prayer I guarantee He will answer, because He always underwrites His Son's requests. And the Lord Jesus is right now at His side, telling Him how you feel. "They are weak and life on earth is hard." He knows; He's been here. With a bottle of your numbered tears in His lap, the Lord is your advocate in heaven. And He is asking His Father right now to use His words recorded in John 11 to persuade you that you are still His child.

Agree with your Lord in prayer before you continue.

Father, if it is true that You come near the brokenhearted, I need You now. You know how I feel about this. I can't hide it from You. I don't know if I can go on, and I wonder if You care. I hate to admit it, but I have even doubted Your love for me. I want to believe that I am Your child, but feel like I'm not. Please use the words of Your Son in John 11 to show me where my thinking is wrong and my conclusion flawed. The deepest desire of my heart is to know Your love and to feel Your power in this. I long for Your comfort and care. Encourage me in the pages to come. This may be my last chance to come back to You and the closeness I knew before this tragedy. Please, I beg You, heal my broken heart and give me hope. In Jesus' name, amen.

If you prayed that prayer, you are about to become one of God's very special children. Few Christians will ever appreciate the deep joy and unshakable confidence the Lord is giving you the opportunity to know. He has prepared you for a blessing reserved only for those who hurt. And He is sure to answer your prayer by taking your hand and leading you in the direction you desperately want and need to go.

Chapter 2

DANGEROUS PRAYER

The first lesson God taught me through my affliction was regarding prayer: He taught me the difference between a request and a report. It was an uncomfortable lesson because it required a shift in theology—the same shift I walked a skeptical student through after a class I was teaching at a Christian university.

I had just finished teaching a class on Bible interpretation when she came up to the podium wearing what I call her "Christian frown." Although she was smiling just enough to cover her discomfort with my class, her eyes betrayed her disapproval. Karen was brilliant and dedicated, a model student at our university. When I asked her how I could help her, she gathered her courage. "I disagree with a lot of what you taught today. You took verses out of context and encouraged people in risky ways. I would never pray like you told us to pray just now."

Karen objected to one specific line in the lecture: *Stop offering information to the Lord, and start telling Him what you want ... before it's too late.*

"I just feel it's wrong to make Christians think that somehow they could miss something by not asking for it. I pray to talk with God, not to get something from Him," she said. "This idea of having to beg Him for help could cause someone to become dangerously preoccupied with their personal problems."

I opened my Bible to a few of the verses we had studied. "I know many who agree with your fear that this teaching is dangerous," I said. "Read these words with me and answer me this. Is it my teaching or the passage itself that is dangerous?"

Reminding her of our firm commitment to a literal interpretation—that the Bible can never mean what it never meant—I turned to these sentences, asking her what she thought they meant to the disciples who first heard them.

The first verse I asked her about was James 4:2: "What does James mean when he says, 'You do not have because you do not ask'?"

She just stared at the page, so I stated the obvious.

"Doesn't this raise the possibility of not receiving something God wants to give you because you did not take advantage of your privilege to ask for it?"

Still no answer, so I directed her to Mark 11:24.

"After picturing what faith in God can do with the impossible feat of casting an enormous mountain into the sea, Jesus says, 'Therefore I say to you, whatever things you ask when you pray, believe that you receive them, and you will have them.'"

I had underlined three words as I read—*things, ask, believe.* "Karen, you seem uncomfortable with all three," I said. "But the Lord's advice is to *ask* for whatever specific, definite *things* are on your heart, and *believe* that He will do the impossible."

"How do you get 'tell Him what you want before it's too late' from this?" She seemed to concede the need to *ask* for *something* in *faith.*

"Karen, do we need to turn back to James 4:2? It's not my words but God's words that are making you uncomfortable. Would you mind if we made this a little more personal and less academic?" I asked.

"What do you mean?" She seemed fearful.

"Karen, if you could ask God for anything right now, what mountain would you ask Him to cast into the sea? Think of that one thing in your life you would ask Him to deliver you from," I said. "What heartache, fear, or disappointment is breaking your heart right now?"

I could tell a very specific crisis or sorrow was on her mind.

"The Lord Jesus knows what you are thinking right now," I pressed. "It would take us hours to review all the conversations about prayer He had with His followers. They all speak of urgency—*keep asking, seeking, knocking; My Father wants to give you good things; ask in My name.* The early leaders of the church heard Him. Peter and Paul constantly begged their followers to pray for them."

I reminded her again of James 4:2: "You do not have because you do not ask."

"What is your mountain?"

Karen looked at the floor. "My parents are getting a divorce, and I won't be able to come back to school next semester. They don't have the money," she said quietly.

I handed her a napkin to wipe her tears. "Ask the Lord before it's too late, Karen. Beg Him to let you stay here with your friends," I told her. "You never know. He may cast that mountain into the sea. But you must *ask!*"

Before I got sick, Christians never seemed uncomfortable with my teaching on prayer. It was "safe," the usual. But on the night I almost died, a revered mentor named Charlie White prayed for me in a dangerous way—and I lived.

Like Karen, and like me before her, millions of hurting Christians are afraid to pray dangerous prayers of faith. They've never known this type of excruciating pain before. They believe that God loves them. They want to pray. But the words in their hearts scare them.

Are you afraid to ask the Lord to cast your mountain into the sea? If so, I want to introduce you to a family in the tiny Judean town of Bethany on the day their world fell apart. Like the many believers who picked up this book, this family has suffered a great tragedy. As you get to know the family members better, I believe you will easily identify with their personal experience. Their names are Martha, Mary, and Lazarus.

> ARE YOU AFRAID TO ASK THE LORD TO CAST YOUR MOUNTAIN INTO THE SEA?

John introduces us to their story in the eleventh chapter of his gospel. Lazarus is very sick, and Martha and Mary are becoming despondent as they debate whether to send for Jesus in their time of need.

TAKING CARE OF GOD

The apostle begins by making sure we know exactly which family he is talking about. It is Wednesday in Perea on the east side of Jordan when the couriers arrive. But John's extended description of this special household takes us behind the scenes—back west, a twenty-four-hour journey across the Jordan to Bethany, where suddenly it was Lazarus's last day.

Waking from a fitful sleep on Tuesday morning, Mary and Martha move to their brother's bedside. Lazarus's condition has not changed, and they have been up with him many times throughout the night. They long for the slightest sign of improvement. Is he more alert? Does he seem more comfortable? Has his fever broken?

Standing over his pathetic form, they know immediately that his time is short. Death came often to the streets and homes of Judea in the first century. The smell of death was in the room, the tint of death in his face.

Alarmed, the women wipe his forehead with a cool cloth. "Lazarus, wake up. Lazarus, the morning has come. Open your eyes. Lazarus, you must wake up." But their brother is too weak to hear their voices.

"*He's dying!*" Martha cries. "Time is running out, Mary. We must send for the Lord now. He is our only hope!"

The question had been on their hearts for days as their brother's condition worsened. "Should we send for Jesus?"

Right now, the answer to that question seems obvious to us: *Yes! Send for Jesus!* we think. But times were much different back then. In fact, Lazarus may have told them not to send for Jesus because of the danger. Jesus' last two visits to the city had stirred the people in ways that threatened His enemies, and they had turned on Him with murderous rage. It was only a short time earlier that Jesus had stayed with them following the tumultuous events of the Feast of Tabernacles (Luke 10:38–42). The plot to kill Him was known even to the people who suspected the rulers' self-preserving motives. "Can it be that the authorities really know that this is the Christ?" (John 7:26 ESV).

Jesus fled for His life to another Bethany, east of the Jordan River, beyond the reach of the Jewish authorities. There, in the province of Perea, where John the Baptist preached, and where Jesus met His first disciples, Jesus' ministry flourished.

As their brother fades, the sisters agonize over their choice. Should they bother Jesus with their personal problems? What a selfish mistake it would be to distract the Lord from His mission and put His life at risk.

But Lazarus has not improved. He is worse, much worse. Death is near.

Mary looks at Martha. "Send for the runners. Now!"

THE REPORT

The two desperate sisters give careful but hurried instructions to the men who will carry the news of Lazarus's condition to Jesus. They must have believed *everything* depended on these messengers. "Go straight to the Lord. Do not linger here or loiter on the way. And tell Him exactly what we say to you, word for word: 'Lord, behold, he whom You love is sick'" (John 11:3).

John makes sure we are aware of just how special these people were to Jesus:

> Now a certain man was sick, Lazarus of Bethany, the town of Mary and her sister Martha. It was that Mary who anointed

> the Lord with fragrant oil and wiped His feet with her hair, whose brother Lazarus was sick. (John 11:1–2)

His introduction refers to a famous event that heightens our appreciation of this family's relationship with Jesus in two ways:

1. They were close to Jesus. Everyone knew of Jesus' special attachment to this family. Their comfortable house, just a few miles from the city, became His personal refuge during His visits to Jerusalem. He felt a rare freedom in their home. Luke pictures Jesus relaxed and at ease with them. He even helps them settle family disputes (Luke 10:38–42). Of all the homes in Judea, the Lord chose this one. Their openhearted hospitality gave Jesus access to their lives so that He could truly abide there.

2. They were devoted to Jesus. Mary's extravagant worship of Jesus the week before His death (John 12:1–8) was well known years later when John wrote his gospel. This was no ordinary anointing. Her spontaneous expression of gratitude and compassion revealed a deep love that is precious to the Lord.

I love the images that come to my mind when I read about this family. Jesus finishes a long day in Jerusalem. He is absolutely spent. Finally, as He turns southeast on the road to Bethany, a smile. Just two more miles and He will be there. He knocks on the door. Only once. Mary has been awaiting His arrival. "Martha, it's Him. It's the Lord!" she announces. Martha calls from the kitchen, "I've made Your favorite meal. Lazarus has prepared Your room, just the way You like it." Jesus falls into the most comfortable seat in the home and, for the first time since His last stay, totally relaxes.

For years I read this introduction to the story of Lazarus never noticing the jarring disconnect between verses 2 and 3. With the images from Bethany in mind, the message the sisters sent to Jesus just doesn't make sense:

> Therefore the sisters sent to Him, saying, "Lord, behold, he whom You love is sick." (John 11:3)

This isn't a prayer; it's a report!

Why would these women, as close to Jesus as you can get, make no specific request? What were they thinking?

In just a few hours they will rehearse every decision they have made in this crisis over and over. Only God knows if the sisters wished they had sent Jesus more than their one-sentence memo that morning.

From what we know about this family, I think they did. I know I would have. "Lazarus is dying, ladies," my heart cries today as I read verse 3. "And you're sending Jesus information!"

If I were standing outside Martha and Mary's house in Bethany that day, I know now what I would tell them before they sent their message to Jesus:

"Jesus is your Friend. He loves you like no other," I would remind them. "Don't send Lazarus's *medical report* to Him; beg Him *to come* to you. Plead with the Lord for the life of your brother—before it's too late. Or you'll wish you had and be sorry for the rest of your life. Don't *tell* Him about your problem; *ask* Him to help you!"

If you think I'm being a little hard on the two sisters, I'm going to ask you to put yourself in their place. John's record of their tragedy shifts to Perea in verses 4–16, but Mary and Martha have to go back into the house.

Let's walk with them to the deathbed, where reports to Jesus suddenly seem foolish and missed opportunities fill our hearts with regret.

Oh, Lazarus

We know that Lazarus died shortly after the messengers left for Perea—a journey of about twenty-four hours. One day to Perea to bring the news to Jesus, two more days there as the Lord waited (John 11:6), and one day for Jesus and His entourage to come to Bethany. That's four days; the same four days Martha would later remind the Lord that Lazarus's remains had been decomposing (v. 39).

Exactly when the sisters realized that their report to the Lord no longer mattered we can only guess. But it was soon after they bid the runners off that crisp spring morning.

Can you picture them entering into the still air of the house and stopping by the figure lying in bed? I imagine them explaining themselves to their brother. "Lazarus, we just couldn't wait. We sent word to Jesus. He needs to know how sick you are. It's just too hard watching you suffer so. He'll know what to do."

"Lazarus?" Mary repeats. "Lazarus …"

"Lazarus?" Martha throws back the cover and rolls him on his back.

"Lazarus!" She holds his lifeless hand in hers and looks up at her sister. There is no need to mouth the words. He is gone.

"Oh, Lazarus!" Mary cries as she cups his head in her hands. She gazes into her brother's eyes for any sign of life, and her tears wet his face. She wipes them with her hair.

"Oh, Lazarus, why did we wait? We should have sent for the Lord sooner. What were we thinking? He could have saved you. But now it's too late."

It's interesting to me that they never sent Jesus an update: "Never mind, Lord. Lazarus died shortly after the first messengers left."

They had plenty of time. Jesus didn't make a move for forty-eight hours after receiving the initial report. Jerusalem is still a dangerous place for the Lord. Surely they would want to warn Him against making a useless trip now. After all, he's dead! "Hurry! Tell Jesus of Lazarus's death. It's too late to help him now. Jesus must stay in Perea."

Nothing. No warning. Not even a death announcement.

Anguish—when the worst you can imagine happens—sure does change your priorities and opinions.

It sure transformed my view of prayer the night I almost died.

DYING IN LOS ANGELES

Like Lazarus and his sisters, Judy and I talked about the Lord and sent reports to Him when I was on the way to my deathbed.

February in Southern California can be spectacular, one of our favorite times of the year. This February seemed especially encouraging. We loved what God was doing in our church. The "corner" we seemed so bent on turning looked closer than ever before.

"This is no time to get the flu," I remember saying to Judy on

Friday night as we drove to my daughter's house in central California. The next morning my knee swelled to the size of a small watermelon. I took some home remedies and preached on crutches that Sunday.

Every medical professional in the congregation scolded me for not seeing a doctor. I promised them I would first thing Monday morning.

"Mr. Underwood, you're in trouble," the doctor told me the next day. "Your knee implant is infected. I'm sending you to a surgeon at USC who specializes in this procedure."

Looking out my hospital window at the medical center, I could see Dodger Stadium. *At least I have a nice view,* I thought as I briefed the Lord again concerning my situation: *Lord, You know my schedule. This needs to go quickly. I have to be out of here by the end of the week.*

My journal entries the two weeks following my surgery read like a military duty log:

> 24 February: *Today I go to surgery. Lord, help me to love Judy well during this time. I need to face this with courageous faith.*
>
> 29 February: *I go home this afternoon. Father, teach me the lessons of faith You have for me in this. Show me how to share these insights with the elders and staff.*
>
> 10 March: *Feeling a little weak today. I need more strength.*
>
> 20 March: *Can't get out of bed. I need to get better so I can preach on Sunday.*

Lazarus would have been proud of me. I was careful not to ask the Lord for anything personal. It was all about the Lord and His work.

Mary and Martha would have agreed with my concise updates to the Lord Jesus concerning my medical status. Until the day time ran out and Lazarus died with their report still on its way to Perea.

TIME IS RUNNING OUT!

I knew something was terribly wrong several weeks after the surgery when I caught my image in the mirror. Able only to lift my head, I was repulsed by the face staring back at me. Swollen, yellow, hideous. "That can't be me! Lord, what is happening to me?"

When Judy came home a few hours later, she took one look and rushed me back to University Hospital. I could hear the doctors as I faded in and out.

"Acute renal failure."

"Toxic shock."

"Extremely critical."

I was dying.

Family and friends soon arrived and gathered around my bed. Most couldn't bear to look at me. A few offered to pray.

Father in heaven, we come to You now with full confidence that You are the Sovereign of the universe. Every circumstance of our life is under Your watchful eye. So now we trust You as the One who knows best—the God who never makes mistakes. Give us the faith to endure in this confusing and difficult time.

As they prayed, I looked around the room. My son, on leave from his duties as an army officer, held his mother and sister with his wife at his side. The picture of their grief just didn't fit with the prayers being offered in that desperate room.

Father, Your Son, Jesus, sits at Your right hand, and we come to You in His name. Please hear our prayer as we submit to Your will. Though we may not understand this, You know all things. We praise Your majestic name.

I had prayed these prayers myself, many times. At bedsides and in emergency rooms all over this country I had offered reports to God with theological precision. Though absolutely sincere in my motivation to comfort the broken lives I prayed for, I somehow felt a responsibility to pray in a way that protected God.

Like the student I told you about earlier, Christians who actually asked God for something in faith and expected Him to answer made me feel uncomfortable. Like her, my role had always been to pray for others who may have lost perspective in a tragedy.

But on that day I realized the enormous difference between standing at someone's deathbed and lying in your own.

Stop telling God what He already knows! I wanted to shout. *Look at my wife, my children. I'm dying and you're preaching on the sovereignty of God? Somebody ask Him for something. There's not enough faith in this room to heal a bunny rabbit!*

Time was running out.

LET THIS BOY LIVE!

Just then our elders walked into the room. Even they were shaken by the tortured figure in the bed that eerily resembled their pastor.

Charlie White, mentor to most of us in the room and friend to all, taught us a lesson in prayer at that moment. Leaning across my bed like a prophet of old, this dear brother cried out to His God:

> *Father, we are frail and foolish. There is little here we comprehend. But we remember Your love for us and hear the words of Your Son who taught us to pray. He promised us You would listen to our prayers and that He would remind You that we are weak. He told us to pray with the faith of a mustard seed, to believe that You are able to answer our prayers. He told us that with You all things are possible. And so, our Father, we come now to Your throne of grace with this one request: Please heal our pastor. O Lord, we love him and do not want him to die. There is so much to do. Our church needs him; his family needs Him. Please let him live. We beg You, in Jesus' name.*

And then, his own private appeal: "Lord, I love Ed. Please let this boy live and serve. Amen."

The fear and doubt drained from my heart as this old saint and retired pastor spoke his mighty prayer. His bold words gave us hope. His faith kindled a fire of courageous faith that spread around the world. By the next day, over ten thousand Christians were repeating Charlie's simple request: *Please let Ed live and serve.*

As a man of the Word, Charlie seemed intensely alert to the excesses we should avoid when we encourage prayers of faith:

1. God will never do something contrary to His sovereign will. Charlie's humility before God's throne did not presume to know better than his all-knowing Father.

2. When God does respond to prayer, it is never because we demand our answer according to some formula or with enough faith that forces His hand. The seasoned elder was not claiming anything except the love and power of his Father Almighty, and the promises of Jesus, His Son.

3. God loves His children and delights in caring for them. In my time of need, this retired pastor known throughout Southern California as a spiritual giant spoke before the throne of heaven in childlike sentences, appealing to the heart of his Abba Father.

You can say what you want. I believe Charlie's prayer saved my life.

He asked. And God said, "Yes!"

Have you asked?

Or is your fear of what others might think holding you back from the threshold of God's throne of grace?

Stop worrying about how your prayers sound to Christians, and start begging God for what you want and need. He's waiting to hear your bold and dangerous prayer of faith.

This is a book about suffering. In the next chapter you will discover that my anguish was just beginning. As with Mary and Martha, the excruciating pain I was going through was about to bring me to the brink of faith and raise a question in my mind about Jesus and His love.

Before we move on, I encourage you to kneel before your Abba Father. Tell Him exactly *how* you feel and *what* you want. Don't suffer unnecessarily for one more minute. What a waste it would be for you to miss the comfort He wants you to have. All because you did not ask!

Charlie is in heaven now, but his mighty cry is your encouragement. Follow his lead; pray his risky prayer of faith, filling in the details of your personal request:

> *Father, I am frail and foolish. There is little here I comprehend. But I remember Your love for me and hear the words of Your Son, who taught me to pray. He promised me that You would listen to my prayers and that He would remind You that I am weak. He told me to pray with the faith of a mustard seed, to believe that You are able to answer my prayers. He told me that with You all things are possible. And so, my Father, I come now to Your throne of grace, with this one request: Please ________ __________. I beg You, in Jesus' name. Amen.*

If I may be so bold, before you get up from your knees, would you pray for me? You see, I really believe what I just wrote. My doctors still wonder at the power of this prayer against my disease. They tell me "it wouldn't hurt" to keep asking friends to pray: *Father, please let Ed live and serve.*

Thank you. Your daring and dangerous prayer comforts my heart and gives me hope.

Chapter 3

WHY NOT ME?

Have you ever been disappointed by someone you thought cared for you deeply? Just when you needed that person most, he or she failed you.

Initially you resist feelings of disappointment and betrayal. *I'm just being too sensitive. I shouldn't be thinking these horrible things about my friend.*

You wonder why that person suddenly seems so disinterested. *Is this a bad time? Maybe we're not as close as I thought.*

Then your need turns to crisis—what you feared most happens. Still, no word from your friend.

In your heart you know that if your friend ignores you now, your relationship will never be the same.

What if that person who is letting you down is Jesus? Would your feelings of disappointment go deeper? Where would you turn with your suspicions and fears? At that moment, when what you dreaded most actually occurs, what thoughts would you have about the friend you were sure would never let you down?

Is it possible that Jesus isn't aware of your situation? Is He ignoring your grief? I've met many Christians who consider such doubts heretical or weak. They imagine that they would never feel this way about their Lord.

You may have thought that way before your personal calamity. Now you feel ashamed of the one question churning in your heart.

Like Mary and Martha, you must admit that your prayers could have been bolder. But still, isn't there something to be said for faithfulness? You may have heard stories of healing and deliverance from other Christians. Your New Testament is full of such stories—Jesus giving sight to the blind, healing the sick, feeding thousands, and telling the lame to walk!

If it's true that the Lord can do these things for others, then how do you explain His seeming indifference to your need? These feelings you don't want to admit—even to yourself—burn, flaring up with every memory or report of His care for others.

Your troubled heart cries for help. "Please, Lord, I don't want to doubt You. Send me someone, anyone, to make this easier for me to understand."

When that person shows up, you wonder if Jesus misunderstood your prayer.

WITH FRIENDS LIKE THESE

As John shifts the story from Bethany to Perea, he recalls the Lord's immediate reply to the sisters' report:

> When Jesus heard that, He said, "This sickness is not unto death, but for the glory of God, that the Son of God may be glorified through it." (John 11:4)

If you know anything about followers of Christ, you can easily imagine what happened when Jesus said that.

We know that the disciples interpreted Jesus' sentence to mean that there was no need for them to go back to that dangerous place. Mary and Martha had nothing to worry about. Everything would be just fine. Just take Jesus at His word and give Lazarus a little time to rest (John 11:12).

Just a few months earlier, these same men had heard the Lord explain a beggar's blindness in the same way. When asked why this pitiful street person was chosen to live all his days in darkness, Jesus replied, "That the works of God should be revealed in him" (John 9:3).

And what a work of God the Lord Jesus revealed on that day! He did something that had never been done before, not in all the history of Israel—He healed a blind man (John 9:7).

Assuming that they fully understood the Lord's words, Jesus' disciples falsely concluded that Lazarus was not going to die. Later Jesus would tell them plainly that His friend was already dead (John 11:14), and they would come to realize that what Jesus really meant was that all of this would not end with Lazarus still in the grave.

But all the disciples could think about at the moment was the good news Mary and Martha needed to hear. Or was it the good news *they needed to give*?

"Well, you heard the Lord," one of them must have said to the couriers. "Hurry back to Bethany. Tell Lazarus's sisters that this is all for the glory of God and that he will get better. Just stay strong. It will all work out; you'll see. It's all good."

We hear that far too often, don't we?

People come to our dark places of anguish with words far easier to say than to live. If those people are Christians, their words probably sound like this: "And we know that all things work together for good to those who love God, to those who are the called according to His purpose" (Rom. 8:28).

Like the disciples in Perea, these people are just trying to help. Presuming that they know how this promise would comfort people like us, they quote it without thinking. "Don't worry," they said with a smile. "This will all work out for good, you'll see. Just trust Jesus ... and get some rest."

If they only knew we're really thinking when we answer, "That's right. Just trust Jesus."

The Question

The Lord Jesus rescued me in such a dramatic way that I thought I would never doubt Him. I was an angry young man losing my way when I met the Savior. The revival now known as the Jesus Movement brought His words of hope to thousands of people who had never trusted religion. We were the rebels of the sixties, but God's grace melted our hearts and turned us to our Savior. We met Jesus on the streets and campuses of America, and then walked those same streets and campuses telling everyone about our new Friend.

But here I was, thirty years later, wondering if He really cared as my skin fell from my burning and weakening body and the best doctors in the nation couldn't figure out why. Before this, I thought my knee infection was suffering at its worst. Now I know better.

When friends encouraged me to trust Him, I struggled, afraid to tell them of a most troubling question festering in my heart.

"Why not me?"

I remember the night we prayed for a young man the doctors said had only a few hours to live. He was a nominal Christian living a self-absorbed life. God healed him, yet he still walked away from the faith. All I want to do is serve Him. *Why not me?*

I know a few immoral pastors who have damaged God's reputation and destroyed churches. In His grace God has given them many "second" chances. All I want is one. *Why not me?*

I have friends who fall apart and openly challenge God's goodness if they don't get the promotion, their vacation is disappointing, or the dryer breaks. God tenderly leads and nurtures them in spite of their demanding spirit. I just want to live. *Why not me?*

You save others, Lord. *Why not me?*

You take such good care of everyone else. *Why not me?*

I can almost hear some of you objecting, "I would never say that to Jesus!" Don't be so sure. Sincere Christians just like you have tried to push this question to the back of their minds and "just trust Jesus."

It never works.

Suppressing the question is not the solution. Lying to your Savior when your heart screams for more only intensifies the pain. Earnest Christians who attempt to hide their hurt from Christ are trapped in a dark room of despair. They feel little of the comfort they hear others speak of, and they don't know why.

Are you one of those still holding out? Afraid of the question, have you confused the disingenuous denial of the disappointed with the faith and strength of the mature? You need to ask the question.

If you don't ask Him why, you'll never know the comfort in His answer. But you must ask Him sincerely. And in the same way that Jesus came to rescue the faith of Mary and Martha, He will come to you with tender care and loving words of healing.

I understand your situation may not be the same as mine. Perhaps you are not dealing with a physical ailment or the illness of a loved one, and so you don't think this question applies to your situation. But the truth is, any number of circumstances might cause us to distrust God's goodness. This is the question of the faithful when we don't understand what's happening. Here are some other examples of what this might look like. See if any of these situations might apply to you:

THIS IS THE QUESTION OF THE FAITHFUL WHEN WE DON'T UNDERSTAND WHAT'S HAPPENING.

- Other women treat their husbands with contempt, but You sustain their marriages through the chaos of their ungodly lives. I have given my husband every respectful and submissive expression of love You ever guided me toward, yet he just moved in with his coworker. You take such good care of other families—why not my kids? *Why not me?*

- I have tightened my belt for years so that I could submit to You in my finances. How many times have I passed on buying something for myself or even my loved ones so that I could devote to You the portion of my money I thought You desired? I did this with the purest motivation I could muster as Your Word encouraged me, "as the cheerful giver You love." So this is how You show Your love? My partner embezzled the last penny from our business and I can't make payroll! Lawyers and debt collectors are after me, and I'm going to lose it all—my retirement, my home, my future. You seem so careful to keep so many irresponsible believers afloat. You intervene with sudden and dramatic gifts and financial windfalls. These people are at best casual, spontaneous, and inconsistent givers, yet You underwrite their irresponsibility. *Why not me?*

- Lord, I've taken care of myself with an intensity most of Your people will never know. Up early, eating right, working out like a madman. I never abuse alcohol or drugs, and I ask for health for the eternally significant reason of a dedicated disciple—I just want to serve You with sound mind and body. But I'm the one with cancer. I have watched You help those who are terrible stewards of their earthly bodies and marveled at Your willingness to give them years and even decades of health. You seem so ready to encourage them physically and give them hope. *Why not me?*

- Ours is a Christian home, a loving home. All we want to do is raise our children so that they will make a difference for You in this world. We take them to church,

> talk to them about You, read Bible stories, and try to show them how Christ can make a difference in their lives. And now my baby is sick, and the doctors tell me there's nothing they can do. Some of our friends ignore their children. They work long hours and hardly ever come to church. They're too busy for You or their family. But their children are a picture of health. You take such great care of them. *Why not me?*

With that simple, heartfelt question, you enter the world of the two sisters left alone in Bethany. When what you hear and read about the Lord's care and concern for others causes you to doubt His commitment to you, think about how Lazarus's sisters must have felt. They were eyewitnesses to the miracles of Christ. They had taken Him into their home when the entire city had turned against Him!

Like you, these two faithful followers of Jesus must have wondered if He really cared. And if He did, why had He let them down in the time of their greatest need?

Unlike you, Mary and Martha could not read on in John's inspired defense of the love and wisdom of their Master. In the next few verses, John explains what he and the other disciples had missed when Jesus announced His plan to go to Lazarus.

AN APPOINTMENT WITH GLORY

As I read verse 4, I sense the beloved disciple's intensity as he pens the words. John is an old man by the time he actually writes his gospel, and he has told the story of Lazarus hundreds of times to audiences all over the New Testament world. Their reaction to this point has always been the same.

"What possible reason could Jesus have had for letting Lazarus die? He once healed a royal official's son in Capernaum without even leaving Cana. He simply spoke the words, 'Your son lives,' and at that very moment the boy's fever left him (John 4:46–54). If He could heal a stranger's son from over ten miles away, surely He could heal one of His closest friends from a distance!"

I suspect that Mary and Martha had told John of their own struggle with these questions. If Jesus only needed to speak the words and Lazarus would be healed, then why didn't He speak them?

Does this describe your thoughts? Does it correspond to the emotions you have when your heart cries out, *Why not me?* Mercifully, your feelings were on John's mind as he selected the most important sentences from Mary and Martha's conversations with Jesus that day.

John would not want you, or anyone else, to think that Jesus trifled with His followers. Carefully, he writes down Jesus' words, exactly as He spoke them so long ago: "This sickness is not unto death, but for the glory of God, that the Son of God may be glorified through it" (John 11:4).

Then John checks back in his account of Jesus' life to be sure he has accurately characterized the magnitude of Jesus' words. The disciple is looking for a similar sentence he had recorded earlier, after Jesus' first year of ministry, when He had commanded a cripple to pick up his mat and walk on the Sabbath. We know it today as John 5.

Jesus kept referring to God as His own Father, and then the

Lord said this: "Most assuredly, I say to you, the hour is coming, and now is, when the dead will hear the voice of *the Son of God*; and those who hear will live" (John 5:25).

Reading it again, the aged apostle remembers the astonished looks among Jesus' band of followers. "Did you hear what He just said?" their eyes asked one another. "Did He say *Son of God?*"

It was the only other time Jesus said it—ever—until He began preparing His disciples for the lesson they would learn through Lazarus's pain.

> "This sickness is not unto death; but for the glory of God, that the *Son of God* may be glorified through it." (John 11:4)

Without explaining Himself further, Jesus told them that the events surrounding Lazarus's sickness would reveal His glory as the Son of God.

Could it be that part of the answer to your question *"Why not me?"* is that Jesus is doing something more wonderful than you ever imagined? Is it possible that your heartache is designed to bring glory to the Savior in a way so unique and breathtaking that this is the only way? That's John's point: Jesus never messes with His followers.

WHEN WE BEGIN TO DOUBT HIS WISDOM, WE NEED TO THINK ABOUT HIS GLORY. WHEN WE BEGIN TO DOUBT HIS CARE, WE NEED TO THINK ABOUT HIS LOVE.

When we begin to doubt His wisdom, we need to think about His glory.

When we begin to doubt His care, we need to think about His love.

Assurance of Love

Over the years, one objection to the story of Lazarus's death had especially bothered John. "How cruel of Jesus to leave Mary and Martha in doubt. He knew Lazarus was already dead, and He knew He was going to call him from the grave. Why didn't He give the couriers *that* message? If He really loved Mary and Martha, He would have told them plainly!"

I picture John, the devoted friend of Jesus, pausing as he forms the next sentence in his mind:

> So, when He heard that he was sick, He stayed two more days in the place where He was. (John 11:6)

Obviously, John knew that this was exactly how it happened. The disciples had understood Jesus to mean that Lazarus was not going to die, but that He would be glorified as the Son of God, so they waited around for *two more days.*

John anticipates the effect of these words on the reader because of the reaction to Jesus' seemingly slow response to Lazarus's death:

"Two days! Why wait?" the reader has asked John. "Even if Jesus needed to make sure Lazarus's body had decomposed to prove the miracle, He could have started for Bethany immediately. Mary and

Martha needed Him right away. If He really loved them, He would not have delayed!"

All of us who ask the question "Why not me?" have had these thoughts. *If Jesus really loved me, He would come to my side quickly and tell me plainly.*

A very special friend of ours wondered about God's love for her. A pastor's wife for over twenty years, her world fell apart when a young woman in the church exposed her husband's secret life.

When the pastor confessed his infidelity, our friend tried to follow God's guidance in every detail. Assuring her husband of her continued devotion to him and their marriage, she went to counseling, listened to advice from friends and leaders of the church, and dedicated her total efforts to any suggestion for saving their marriage. She went on a diet, demanded that the children respect him, confessed her shortcomings, tried to communicate better, gave him more sex—if God's Word said it, she did it.

Continuing his double life, her husband never came around. With every disappointment, her despair deepened. *What is God doing? What does He want me to do?*

She remembers her conversations with the Lord after the divorce—her marriage was gone; her church was gone; her life would never be the same.

"I cried every morning on the freeway driving to my first real job in decades. Suddenly I was part of the secretary pool. I parked in the back to wipe my tears and put on my makeup. *Lord, why won't You help me? Why are You making this so hard?*

Why didn't You just have him leave me when I first found out? What possible reason do You have for making this into such a trying and long process? And why won't You just tell me what to do?"

Jesus lingered only two days in Bethany. Our friend struggled through her process with no answers *for years.*

Years ago, a man with advanced multiple sclerosis came to our church. When he told me that he had no hope in life, I told him about Jesus. This man placed his faith in Jesus, and it has made every difference in his spiritual and emotional life.

Jesus has restored his marriage, provided many loving friends, and given him opportunities to tell others about God. His life is fuller and more meaningful than most totally healthy men his age.

But he is still trapped in a body that refuses to cooperate, and he becomes a little more dependent on others every day.

Mary and Martha only had to wait a few days for Jesus' answer to their pain. This dear man has been walking with God for nine years with no physical improvement.

Could it be that God's silence in these matters means that Jesus somehow does not love these people as much as others? As we return to the passage, one clarifying sentence interrupts the flow of the story with emphatic assurance that this simply is not true:

> Now Jesus loved Martha and her sister and Lazarus. (John 11:5)

John wants us to be assured of Jesus' love for His friends. John not only chooses the special term *agape* to describe Jesus' love, but he also uses the most picturesque tense of the verb, the imperfect tense, which describes the way things *always were*. John is telling us that every time Jesus had the opportunity to express or demonstrate His love for this family, He did.

Rather than just saying, "Jesus loved this family," John takes time to name them one by one, beginning with Martha, the head of the household: "This deep love was for each one of them—Martha *and* her sister *and* Lazarus."

As Jesus' closest friend, John could not bear to think that anyone would conclude that Jesus' delay was due to His lack of affection for His followers.

While the disciples relaxed in Perea, Jesus' mind was on His friends in Bethany. His personal devotion to each of them never wavered. Their feelings were in His heart, and His eye was on their lives. Nothing missed His loving gaze.

So, how long did you have to wait in confusion before you began wondering about Jesus' love for you? When did you start fearing that the answer to your question "Why not me?" might be "Because I do not love you!"

You may not fully understand all of the reasons for what seems like Jesus' undue delay and what all of this means, but you can be sure of what it doesn't mean: It does *not* mean that He doesn't love you.

If your pain has caused you to wonder if Jesus' love for you has diminished or even stopped altogether, read that sentence again in the present tense with your name written into it instead of Martha's and Mary's: "Now Jesus loves ________________________."

Close your eyes, and repeat those words over and over again.

Our need to feel Christ's love for us right now is greater than we know. It is the one constant in our lives that we cannot live without.

I believe that suffering believers, more than any others, need to have a simple, childlike faith in Jesus' love like the one expressed in the familiar hymn: "Jesus loves me this I know, for the Bible tells me so."

Ask Him for the strength of faith you need right now to believe that this is true for you. Tell Him that your *"Why not me?"* confusion is clinging to His *"I love you"* assurances by a thread. Ask Him to come to you now and renew your confidence in His love.

Glory and Love

It's been a number of years since people gathered around my hospital bed with troubled faces and self-conscious words, but I can still feel the desperate sense of betrayal. I can still picture the IV drips plugged into both arms. I can still hear the incessant beeping of the medical equipment. I can still smell the place. I can still feel the helpless confusion of the moment—too weak to speak, too sad to smile. I can still remember the haunting question, "Why not me, Lord?"

What I wish I would have known then is what I'm telling you now.

Whatever you're going through has *something* to do with God's glory. As you look around the hospital room of your life with the helplessness of a person on life support, know that Jesus had something very special in mind when He allowed these circumstances to occur in your life.

Whatever you're going through has *something* to do with God's love. As you see the faces of those trying to help, and you wonder why Jesus takes such good care of them, know that Jesus loves you with the same love He had for you before this happened.

I tried so hard to be kind when people quoted Romans 8:28 to me. I knew they had no idea how much it hurt. "My failing liver is poisoning my body and turning my eyes yellow, and you're telling me to just trust Jesus and get some rest?" I wanted to ask them. "When was the last time you begged God for your next bowel movement, your next breath, to make one more drop of urine? Have you ever wondered if you would get up out of bed again? Make love to your wife? Take your grandson to a ball game? Don't tell me it's all good, because it's not!"

I TRIED SO HARD TO BE KIND WHEN PEOPLE QUOTED ROMANS 8:28 TO ME. I KNEW THEY HAD NO IDEA HOW MUCH IT HURT.

I never asked these questions of friends who kept telling me that everything was going to be just fine when I knew it was only getting worse. I'm glad I didn't because what I realize now as I read on in Lazarus's story is that they were just responding to their Master's call, offering His love in the only way they knew how.

In the next chapter, you'll learn to appreciate Jesus' love for you through your friends' halting and inadequate attempts to ease your pain and give you hope. But I know that you will not read on if you still have real doubts about His love for you.

This will be especially hard if you are beginning to think—or already know—that the answer to your request for healing or relief is *no*. But please keep reading. By the time you finish this book you will learn how the Lord has comforted me through my personal no's—my desperate prayers for the life of a friend and my daily prayers for healing from this disease.

So I'm asking you again. Honestly and with all your heart, tell Jesus that you want to trust His love more. Ask Him, beg Him to energize and strengthen your appreciation of His never-ending love for you. Tell Him you want to believe that He has not abandoned you. Ask Him over and over again, "Why not me?" But let Him know that your protests are peripheral to your foundational and lifelong desire to know His love and relax in His trusting care.

You don't need to hide your hurts from Him; He wants nothing more than to come alongside you as your loving Lord. Here is a prayer I have prayed many times when my doubts clouded my recognition of and response to His tender care all around me:

> *Loving Lord Jesus, You seem to take such great care of others while ignoring my need. I feel left out and marginalized by Your inattention. I don't want to feel this way, but the question on my lips is "Why not me?" Forgive me for thinking this, but You and I know there is no use in my hiding these thoughts from You. So right now, with the faith I've seldom had to call upon, I'm asking Your Spirit to help me trust Your love again. Not forever, just for tomorrow, just long enough for You to speak to my heart and show up in my life in ways that will bring me back to the joy and hope of knowing that I am special to You. Help me trust Your love*

enough to read on, to anticipate the something about Your glory that this must be part of. Lord, I believe, but, as one of the most honest men in the Bible said, I need You to "help my unbelief."

As the Lord answers your prayer and you know that you are trusting His love enough to take the next step, turn the page to discover how His personal care for you may be surrounding you in ways your pain has overlooked.

Chapter 4

LOVE SHOWS UP

Dave and Joni looked forward to the birth of their third child. With two boys bouncing around the house, Joni was thinking how nice it would be to bring home a little girl.

During the delivery, she knew as only a mother can that something was wrong. The doctors and nurses were too quiet. Katie was born with a severe birth defect. Already on her way to heaven, their baby would be with them only briefly. The specialist told them she probably wouldn't make it through the week.

Judy called me in tears, grieving for our dear friends. I called Dave at the hospital to pray with him on the phone. I told him how sad we were to think of them hurting and how helpless we felt.

Ours was a deep friendship, centered in Christ. Dave assured me that he appreciated our love, and then he said something I will never forget. "So many Christians tell me that they don't know what to say. Then they open their mouths and prove it."

Dave's comment came back to me over and over again when it was our lives that were touched by bitter pain. I couldn't believe how hurt I felt by some of the things well-meaning people said. I knew they weren't trying to be mean and wounding, because I had uttered the same words at the bedsides of others.

But at least they had the courage to show up.

The next section of John 11—the decision to return to Bethany of Judea—shows us the two ways God uses the courageous obedience of those who enter a friend's world of pain, even when they do not know what to do or say. The first is a powerful incentive to listen to Jesus when He invites you to follow Him to the side of those who hurt—an experience of intimacy with God you will find nowhere else. The second is a deeper appreciation of the majesty of your risen Lord.

SOME FRIENDS FOLLOW

For two days the disciples felt safe in their understanding of the Lord's response to the sad news from Bethany. Like most Christians, they were uncomfortable with the suffering of friends. They felt a deep need to explain what Jesus was doing and a strange euphoria when their reasoning seemed to mean all was well.

I can almost hear their confident conversation.

"James, how did you sleep last night?"

"Best night's sleep I've had in weeks. I'm just thankful we don't have to go back to Judea. It seems this turmoil is finally over. Good thing we were able to help Mary and Martha by sending that message to Bethany. I hope they're able to trust the Lord to work all this out with Lazarus. How do you think they'll do with all of this, Andrew?"

"Oh, you know Mary. She'll be fine. She's never had a problem listening to the Master. But Martha, now that's a different story. She'll probably give the messengers a bad time. Still, she'll have to understand the will of the Lord in all of this. Someday she'll learn to listen to His words."

John remembers the jarring words of Christ that shook their world:

> Then after this [two days' stay in the place where He was] He said to the disciples, "Let us go to Judea again." (John 11:7)

Dismayed, the men try to hide their fear. The Lord waits for their response. Nobody wants to seem responsible for the toxic doubt polluting the room. The disciples look to the floor, ashamed of what they're thinking. *Why is Jesus asking us to follow Him to that dangerous place if Lazarus isn't going to die?*

So strong was their confusion that John recalls them speaking as one: "Rabbi, lately the Jews sought to stone You, and are You going there again?" (v. 8). The shocked disciples wait for Jesus' reply. As they look into His eyes, a sobering realization begins to settle in their hearts. They have seen this steely look before when their Master determined to confront His enemies. They know Jesus is going on this suicide mission to Bethany. And He's asking them to come with Him.

Don't miss that.

He's *asking* them to follow Him to the bedside of a friend, no matter what the cost. It's not a command but an invitation.

Jesus never forces His people to be with those who hurt. He *asks* us to, even when we don't know what to say or how to act.

I DON'T HAVE THE WORDS

I remember a time when I was on the other side of the suffering equation. It was my first year at Dallas Seminary, and my next-door neighbor, a fellow student, was electrocuted. Judy and I rushed to the hospital to meet friends Wayne and Marie, who also knew the injured man and his wife. Judy and Marie were with his wife when the doctor told Wayne and me that our friend had died.

Wayne and I looked at each other with one of those "you go first" faces you get when the assignment seems ridiculous. *Maybe later, Lord,* was my quick prayer of panic. *After I graduate and it's official. Then I'll know what to say and how to act. I'm just not ready.*

Just then the president of the seminary, Dr. John Walvoord, walked into the room. He was a mountain of a man neither of us had ever seen up close, and his austere presence was at once intimidating, comforting, and delivering.

"How is he, boys?" Dr. Walvoord asked.

"He's dead, sir. The doctor just told us. His wife … I mean, widow, is in there." We pointed, relieved that God had sent an expert and the pressure was off.

I'll never forget this great saint's reply. "What do you say?" he asked us tearfully.

> WE THINK WAY TOO MUCH OF OURSELVES WHEN WE TRY TO OFFER COMFORT IN JESUS' NAME. NOBODY REALLY KNOWS WHAT TO SAY.

We just stared in disbelief as Dr. Walvoord turned toward the door and walked away to comfort this young student's waiting widow.

Wayne and I looked at one another in amazement. We didn't have to say a word. Both of us were silently answering his question the same way: *You are probably the greatest theologian of our day. You've written more books about God than we could ever read. Presidents call you for biblical counsel. And you are asking* us *what to say? Man, if you don't know what to say, nobody does!*

We think way too much of ourselves when we try to offer comfort in Jesus' name. Nobody *really* knows what to say. Nobody *really* knows what to do.

Jesus asks. And we follow.

At His Side

Jesus didn't even try to deny or minimize the dangers facing them in Judea.

He never does. And we wonder why most Christians seem so easily discouraged from following Him. We hate leaving the comfort and security of our understanding.

Jesus wanted His disciples to see *Him*, not the danger. Twice before, Jewish leaders had taken up stones against Jesus (John 8:59; 10:31). Had any of His disciples ever come to any harm? No. Why? Because the Lord was with them!

Knowing that His time with them was short, Jesus encouraged them to make the most of their opportunity to follow Him:

> "Are there not twelve hours in the day? If anyone walks in the day, he does not stumble, because he sees the light of this

> world. But if one walks in the night, he stumbles, because the light is not in him." (John 11:9–10)

Let me restate Jesus' words to the disciples so that we're clear about what He said: "What are you going to do with your time?" Jesus asks. "Come with Me. You will be safer with Me in Judea than you will be on your own here in Perea. Don't waste your time seeking the fleeting security of this world. Your place is with Me, in the light—where you will never stumble."

In just a few days the Lord would gather these same men into the Upper Room to teach them plainly what He is urging them to trust Him for now—the greatest abundance of joy, power, and meaning is found in the presence of the Lord. Those who trust Jesus enough to risk doing His will, especially in the toughest assignments of life, are doing so much more than simply obeying Him. They are choosing to be *with* Him, to remain at His side, to settle in His presence ... to *abide* in Him (John 15:4).

Even as He prepares them for His departure, He will tell them, "You must choose to be near Me. Those who do," He promises, "will know the power of answered prayer as they do great things for Me. But, more important, only those who abide will know the joy of the deepest experience of love with the Son of God—a friendship so close that you will know the deepest truths of My Father" (see John 15:1–15).

When the disciples chose to follow Jesus back to Bethany, they chose to be *near* Him, to *abide* in Him, in the light, where they would never stumble. He was leading them to a place where His people will always experience His presence—particularly those with a broken heart.

Decades later, I'm not surprised at meeting Dr. Walvoord in that emergency room in Dallas. Though we did not know what to say, we knew that the Lord was asking us to do a very difficult thing—to rush to the side of a friend in need. Our obedience was a choice to go where Jesus was going, to abide in Him.

Near the Brokenhearted

When my friend and I followed Christ to the broken heart of this young widow, we were nearer to Jesus. So near that He sent for one of His choicest and most seasoned servants to prove it!

This is a lesson that I have had to relearn over and over in my life. The Lord is near to those who have a broken heart, and those who are with Him will also be near.

> The Lord is near to those who have a broken heart.

A few years ago I was teaching a weeklong study on Colossians at a Bible school and feeling distant from the Lord. Judy and I have been traveling to this small school near the Oregon coast for nearly fifteen years so I can teach this class, and it is usually the highlight of our year as a couple. After walking the spectacular beach and praying together, Judy and I read our devotional. The verse for that day was Psalm 34:18: "The Lord is near to those who have a broken heart."

That's when I knew what was missing—a broken heart! The hurry and pressure of ministry in the months before our "break by the sea" had left little or no room for those whose hearts were breaking. I was so busy *for* the Lord and His people that I had forgotten what it was like to be *with* the Lord and His people, especially those who hurt.

I wept tears of repentance as I walked from our little cottage by the sea to the lecture hall. *Jesus, if You will just show me one broken heart today, I will do my best to come near to that one in Your name. Help me, Lord. I'm not very good at this. I need Your tender Spirit to flow through my words and my life. I know that this is where I will find You.*

I arrived about fifteen minutes early. Outside the entrance was a group of excited and attractive students engaged in lively conversation as they tossed a football around. In a corner of the stage, the student worship team was practicing some new songs for its upcoming trip to area churches. I hated to admit to myself that normally these two gatherings of the up-and-outers of the class would have attracted my attention and my time.

Jesus, of course, would be looking for someone else.

In the third row sat Mary-Beth. About two hundred pounds overweight, she wore old green sweatpants and an almost matching sweatshirt to class. Her desk was a mess of old candy wrappers, empty Coke bottles, and wadded-up paper. She was highlighting every word in Isaiah with a bright green marker. She never looked up.

"Hi, my name is Ed." I walked up to her desk. "I don't believe we've met yet."

"I'm Mary-Beth. That's two names, not just one ... with a hyphen," she said.

"Well, Mary-Beth, you seem very busy. What are you doing?"

She looked down at her Bible. "Ah, studying Isaiah. It's a good book, and the other teacher is teaching it."

"I see. Tell me, who are your close friends in the class? You've been here now for almost nine months. Who do you hang around with? Pray with? Talk to at night when you need some advice or encouragement?"

After Mary-Beth had told me about her mom, her hometown, and many other details of her life, I pressed further. "Sounds like you came from a wonderful home. But back to my question: Who would you consider your closest friends here at school?"

"I don't have any friends," she said. "I don't make friends very easy. People just don't like me much … and that's fine. I kinda get along with everyone."

"Oh, Mary-Beth, that makes me sad," I said. "Everyone needs friends. The body of Christ is one of God's most precious gifts to us here on earth. I couldn't survive without my friends. Would you mind if I prayed for you right now, before class begins? I want to ask the Lord to send you a friend to love you and care for you … someone to bring His joy to your life."

Before she could answer I took the empty seat to her right and began begging God to send her a friend. Just one.

As she buried her sobbing face into my chest, I felt the power and presence of the Lord Jesus that my heart had been searching for. I knew I had found Him next to a lonely, unattractive, overweight young lady in a place filled with "happier" Christians. He was near to her because her heart was broken. And I joined Him there.

> That's what abiding is all about. It's not performing for Christ but being present with Him.

You may be reading this book

because you're wondering if you should go to the side of a friend with a broken heart right now. I urge you to trust Jesus enough to follow. I promise you an experience of God's presence you can find nowhere else.

That's what abiding is all about. It's not performing for Christ but being present with Him. This is what Jesus was teaching His disciples on the day they trusted Him enough to stay with Him all the way to Lazarus's grave.

It's one of the surest ways I know to draw near to God: Find someone with a shattered life and go to him or her in the name of Jesus.

Does your heart long for this type of intimacy with God? Then ask Him to show you your Mary-Beth in the same way I did that day in Oregon:

> *Father, show me one broken heart, and I will do my best to go to it in the name of Jesus. Help me, Lord. I'm not very good at this. I need Your tender Spirit to flow through my words and life. I claim Your promise in Psalm 34:18 that I will find You there. In Jesus' name, amen.*

But there's more.

As you draw near to Jesus in the presence of the hurting, you will see Him in a way most Christians never do.

His Love Shows Up

The evening when it became clear that my body refused to recover from the knee replacement, and my doctors couldn't figure out why, the news began to spread that I was suffering from an unexplainable rash and was near death. So many of my closest friends jumped on planes. They came to my side by the dozens, called by the hundreds, and prayed by the thousands.

They said inane and inappropriate things. They didn't mean to sound shallow or cause pain. It's hard to witness suffering.

But they came.

Many sat in silence. Others cried. A few prayed. They showed up in the name of Jesus and made it better.

I began to see some of the most tangible expressions of Jesus' love for me in the presence of friends.

A nurse from our church skillfully and tenderly rubbed soothing creams into my burning skin night after night. "Sit back and relax, Eddie," she would say. "You're going to be feeling better. I guarantee it."

Lifelong friends from Oregon dropped their lives to bring a message of assurance to my bride: "We'll take care of you if he dies."

Kevin, one of my closest friends, stayed with me the night my liver failed. When the fever broke, he whispered in my ear, "Oh, Ed, your head is so hot. I love you, brother. Jesus is watching this. I'm here. Go back to sleep."

I'm crying like a baby as I put these memories in sentences for you to read. The tears are mixed. Most are tears of joy, but some are tears of repentance.

While demanding the "right words" from my comforters, it never occurred to me that they had volunteered for the mission. I became disillusioned and embittered, maybe—probably—even with Jesus.

If you are reading this book as a sufferer, I have something to tell you that you may not want to hear. But you need to. I know; I've been there. I've thought your bitter thoughts and ascribed your errant motives to Christ and His people. I believe that a major reason for your emotional agony in this crisis may be that you have not seen the love of the Savior in the presence of your friends.

Oh, how He must love you to send them to your side!

They wonder how to act as they knock on your door the day after your wife dies. But His love for you compels them to show up.

When they hear the bad news that your husband confessed adultery, they wish they could think of something profound and helpful. They feel inadequate and foolish. But Jesus moves them to drop everything and come to your side.

They stand with you at the grave of your baby. Not because they have any insight into the theology of death, but because they love you, and Jesus asked them to come.

The sights, sounds, and smells of your hospital room repulse them. They hate seeing you like this. *What does that beeping mean? Is he dying? Why is he so yellow? So hot? So pale? So weak? What are these tubes going into his body? Does my repugnance and apprehension show?* They think someone else would probably do a better job of sitting here with you, but Jesus asked them to come to you.

They come and sit. They cry. They pray.

The people coming to see you are courageously following Jesus' directions. Like Jesus' men on the road back to Judea, they follow when they do not understand.

Think of the questions that must have filled the disciples' minds! *None of this makes sense. Who are we to think we can somehow make a difference here? The Jews have already said they will kill us. And what do I know about medicine? Whatever Lazarus has, I'm no help.*

You see, Jesus was already sending help in His name. I'm sure of it. When He invited the men in Perea to come with Him to help Lazarus, He set a pattern. Your friends' names may not be Nathaniel, James, and John, but they have come at Jesus' bidding. And the same Spirit that moved them to your side is giving you an opportunity to purge your heart of the anger that burdens your soul.

Lord Jesus, forgive me for being so hard on the ones You have sent in Your name. Oh Lord, help me to understand it's not their words but their love that I need. And bring me more … I need them.

My friend, the Lord Jesus has not abandoned you—no more than He abandoned Lazarus and his family. His love and concern is present in the awkward words and unpracticed care of His people.

Not only do you and I need these friends who come in the name of Jesus; they need to be with us. Jesus is calling them to your side not only to be near Him but also to fortify their faith in the crucible of desperation, not only to extend His love but also to experience the grace He extends to them there.

In the next few verses, Jesus teaches Lazarus's friends some lessons of faith they could never learn apart from his suffering. It certainly isn't the "good" they had in mind when they confidently sent the couriers on their way a few days earlier. But it is much of the good Jesus chooses to reveal in suffering.

STRENGTHENED IN FAITH

Tragedy and suffering are never convenient, and they never make sense.

Lazarus's sickness could not have come at a worse time for the disciples. We've already seen how they doubted Jesus' wisdom and questioned His plan. They just could not understand why Jesus would lead them to Judea and certain death.

All Christians cling to notions of independence and strength; we cannot help it. The flesh, like a viral infection of the soul, resists the Spirit's therapy of grace. Only object lessons of Christ's sufficiency at the exact moment we feel most helpless seem powerful enough to convince us that we need Him more than we need a plan.

Jesus loved to teach His followers to trust Him by allowing them to think they understood what He was talking about, when they really had no idea where He was going with a thought. In His last conversation with them before they left for Bethany, Jesus prepared them for what they were about to see by erasing every expectation of personal contribution.

> These things He said, and after that He said to them, "Our friend Lazarus sleeps, but I go that I may wake him up." (John 11:11)

Abruptly Jesus turns the conversation from the dangers along the way back to the friend they will find when they get there. As Hebrews, maybe they should have understood Jesus' euphemism of sleep as an image of death. The Old Testament recorded the death of the patriarchs and kings as a sleep from which there was no earthly awakening—he "*slept* with his fathers" (1 Kings 2:10 ESV). Three of them—Peter, James, and John—had heard Jesus describe the death of a child He raised from the dead with these same words (Mark 5:39).

But now, in Perea, with hearts full of pain and fear, all they hear is "sleep." Like all of us, they immediately downsize the crisis to one they can manage. They actually offer advice to their Master.

"Lord, if he sleeps he will get well." (John 11:12)

Do you hear the desperate attempt for control in those words? This is the last cry of their flesh against the uncertainties and risks of faith. "If that's all it is—a fever—then he will wake up. I've seen it a thousand times. I know exactly what to do. Just wait, Jesus. You'll see. I'll handle this. It's not as bad as it seems. There's no reason to jeopardize our lives just to see a fever break."

Before the self-assured confidence of their lives prior to meeting and walking with Jesus can have its way with them, the Lord tells them plainly, "Lazarus is dead" (v. 14). This simple sentence—these three words, *Lazarus is dead*—takes them to a place they have been trying to avoid. It's not the wilderness of Judea and the streets of Bethany they really fear; it's their absolute powerlessness to really do anything to make the situation better.

Lazarus is dead in Bethany, and if Jesus doesn't do something about it, it's hopeless!

A HARD LESSON

I don't have to imagine the looks on the faces of the disciples when they finally resigned themselves to the awful truth waiting for them at the end of their journey to that dangerous place—their friend was dead and they were powerless to change that.

This is the place Jesus brought those to who gathered together on that dark night in my room on the fourth floor of University Hospital.

It was in the eyes of those who came to "help" us through our tragedy.

The disfiguring power of multiple organ failure was gruesomely obvious to everyone gathered around my bed. One dear lady couldn't contain her horror. Screaming loudly, she ran out in tears.

She left behind a room full of friends who finally got it—I was dying and they could do nothing about it.

The next sentence from Jesus' lips is one of the most surprising in the entire Bible:

> "And I am glad for your sakes that I was not there." (John 11:15)

He is actually *glad* that things have turned out this way. The Greek verb for "I am glad" is often translated "I rejoice" or "I delight in." It expresses *joy*.

Joy over the blank stares of people who just lost hope? *Ed, surely you're not saying that Jesus was actually glad that your friends and loved ones felt useless and despairing?*

I think He was.

I see now what I wish I could have understood then. The events of that night were carefully and sovereignly orchestrated by the Lord Jesus Himself to do a mighty work in the hearts of my friends and loved ones.

If the idea of Jesus rejoicing over our most desperate moments upsets you or makes you feel deceived, alone, and a little annoyed, you're normal! But your annoyance with the Lord will subside when you read the rest of His sentence:

> "... that you may believe." (John 11:15)

That *you,* the ones who will follow Me to the home of our hurting friends, may believe!

What will they believe on this journey from control to courage? They will believe something about Jesus that will change them forever.

From Rabbi to the Son of God

At this precise point we see a striking contrast in John's account of the conversations between the Lord Jesus and His disciples. Before this, they preferred the title *rabbi.*

- The first two who followed asked Jesus, "*Rabbi...,* where are You staying?" (John 1:38)

- "*Rabbi,* eat." (John 4:31)

- "*Rabbi,* when did You come here?" (John 6:25)

- "*Rabbi,* who sinned, this man or his parents, that he was born blind?" (John 9:2)

- And then, finally, the fearful protest of the disciples before they decided to follow Him to Bethany: "*Rabbi,* lately the Jews sought to stone You, and are You going there again?" (John 11:8)

A *rabbi* is someone who speaks in words and teachings you're used to hearing—a *man* of profound insight and wisdom. A *rabbi* could reveal truth, even truth about God. The *rabbis* taught in the synagogue and quoted and compared the teachings of other *rabbis*.

As *Rabbi*, Jesus seemed more comfortable and controllable to His followers, even though His teaching was revolutionary in content and authority (Mark 1:21–28). They could advise their *Rabbi* to eat, ask Him questions, debate His opinions and directions among themselves, even argue with Him.

But these faithful disciples who followed Him to the grave of a friend would never call Jesus *Rabbi* again!

Peter, who was not with the disciples during the events of John 11, later addresses Jesus as *Rabbi* to express his surprise that the fig tree cursed by the Lord withered so quickly (Mark 11:21).

Judas, who viewed Jesus as a failing political figure, would call

Him *Rabbi* to the bitter end. On the infamous night he betrayed the Son of God and first wondered if his *Rabbi* knew of his evil scheme (Matt. 26:25), he finally greeted Jesus as *Rabbi* before embracing Him to identify Him to the arresting soldiers (v. 49).

But not *these* disciples, not the ones who pondered the risks and advisability of following Him to the grief-stricken sisters in Bethany. The events of the next few days would cause John to finally and vigilantly forsake any and every reference to Jesus of Nazareth as a mere *rabbi*.

From this point forward they would refer to Jesus as the *Son of God!*[†]

The dramatic shift at this moment in the gospel of John from referring to Jesus not as *Rabbi* but as the *Son of God* highlights the mighty potential of exactly the type of pain that caused you to pick up this book in the first place. You have continued reading, hoping you'll find some point to this tragedy, some good God can bring from your condition. Well, here it is—some of the good only He can accomplish from your pain:

He wants to use our pain to transform our view of Jesus from a wise "rabbi" we can control to the awesome Son of God we should follow with reverential trust!

We don't like it when we know that there is nothing we can do to help, but Jesus loves it! It's a terrifying place to be, but it is His rare opportunity to show us what He can do without us … as *the Son of God!*

We don't like it when we know that there is nothing we can do to help, but Jesus loves it!

And He rejoices when His people, out of options, finally turn to

Him as God, experience His raw power, and learn to trust Him in a way that will matter for the rest of their lives.

Thomas is the first to let go of any idea of somehow finessing Jesus toward a safe and comfortable plan of action. His melancholy nature expresses what the more optimistic heart has not yet fully grasped.

"Let us also go, that we may die with Him." (John 11:16)

"This is it, then. There is nothing we can do but follow Jesus no matter what … even if it kills us." And it probably will!

And so they go.

Finally accepting Jesus' peculiar invitation to return to Judea now that it is too late (v. 7), they follow Him to Bethany.

But they will never be the same.

Would it help you to know that what your friends see and hear as they gather with the Savior around your pain will strengthen their faith and bring out the best from their hearts? If your answer is yes, then you are closer to understanding some of God's purpose. Close enough to ask for it.

SHOW THEM YOUR SON!

The difference between you and Lazarus, Mary, and Martha is that you can read Lazarus's story. You can know that God uses situations just like yours to exalt Jesus as His one and only Son.

Instead of wondering at your friends' incompetent care for you, you can ask God to use your malady to dramatically transform their ideas about Jesus. Fear and uncertainty are how God prepares hearts for deeper revelations of His Son.

Some may be moved to trust in Him as their Savior. Those already trusting Him for eternal life may learn to trust Him more as Lord.

Could it be that you and your friends, churched and unchurched alike, have lived a life that has kept Jesus safely in the "*rabbi*" box?

Could it be that like most Christians, you and your friends are very familiar with the words of Jesus' teaching but have seldom experienced the touch of His power?

Could it be that coming to your aid will give your friends a front row seat to the mighty power of the Son of God?

I know it could!

In the years since my ordeal, I have heard many of my "care-givers" describe what this touch meant to their lives. Here are a few of their comments:

> Fred, an elder I had mentored in a former church—"This was the first time in my life I prayed such a desperate prayer. I knew that if God didn't save you, you would die. I hate to admit it, but I was actually surprised that you lived. My prayer life will never be the same; I find myself asking God for impossible things and expecting Him to answer more than ever before."

> Darla, abandoned mother of two—"I didn't know how I would face life after my husband left. When I saw how God took care of you and Judy through all of this, it gave me

hope that He could take care of me, too, no matter how much it hurt or how out of control I felt."

Lomorumouy, a young disciple of one of our missionaries from the primitive Daasanach people of northern Kenya—"We [the Daasanach] asked God to help you and Richard [the chairman of my elder board had an accident during one of my hospital stays, and we were both out of action] and Church of the Open Door. And now, here you are. [Richard and I were on a mission trip together a year later to visit our missionaries in Africa.] I don't know how you got here; you just came from the sky. But I am rejoicing that you are here. God is good. We are happy." Then the entire church erupted in celebration.

Daniel, a young businessman—"When the news that you were dying came, it hit me that life could end at any moment. Watching you, your family, and the church beg God to let you live and serve helped me realize that this is exactly what I want to do, serve the Lord with all my strength for all the years He will give me. I turned back to Him and totally rearranged my priorities."

I tell their stories to help you look into the lives of those searching for words and deeds to comfort you from a different perspective—God's. My friend Dave and I still agree that most of us say and do the wrong things when we're trying to help the grieving. But God is teaching us that He is doing much more than we envision when we are in the middle of a personal storm.

As you read on, you'll discover His good words to you personally. But the pages ahead will mean so much more if you have already demonstrated that rare faith that invites the Son of God into the tragedies and tests of life.

Begin the process now by praying this prayer, asking Him to show you the good He meant to display through your tragedy in the faith responses and life changes of those He is sending to care:

Father, You have shown Your love for me by these who have come to my side. I thank You for them and ask You now to make the very most of my pain and their willingness by working powerfully in their lives. Some have never trusted in Your Son. Persuade them to believe. Most have never counted on Him in ways that my dismay has pulled them to. Show me Your glory by the ways You will change them. Help me to think ahead to a time when we will talk about the sure ways You were working when we had lost all hope. In Jesus' name, amen.

---

† Of the twelve disciples, only Nathaniel had ever addressed Jesus as the Son of God. With the declaration of his mentor (John the Baptist) fresh in his heart (John 1:34), and awed by Jesus' knowledge of intimate details of his life, the pure-hearted Galilean exclaimed, "Rabbi, You are the Son of God!" (v. 49).

Except for this one occurrence, the disciples used the tamer title of *Rabbi* when speaking to Jesus. The Jews addressed those who taught the law as *rabbi*, or teacher. Though it was a title of utmost respect, it fell far short of recognition of deity (John 3:2, 26).

When Nathaniel called Jesus the Son of God, he coupled that title with *Rabbi* (John 1:49). Jesus had foretold what they were about to see in Bethany way back then: "If this impressed you," Jesus said, "just wait! Before I'm done with you, Nathaniel, you will see the power of heaven poured out to prove that I am exactly who you said I am—none other than the Son of God" (my paraphrase of John 1:50–51).

Apart from the initial declarations of John the Baptist (1:34) and Nathaniel (1:49), no one had seemed comfortable with the title of Son of God until now. Even the man Jesus healed of blindness appeared hesitant to actually speak the words Son of God (9:35). The convincing evidence surrounding Lazarus's resurrection would glorify Jesus as the Son of God (11:4). Martha's plea for mercy is to the Son of God (11:27); Jesus' enemies' reason for killing Him is His claim to be the Son of God (19:7); and John's ultimate purpose for writing his gospel is to persuade every reader to believe that Jesus is the Son of God (20:31).

Chapter 5

AS BAD AS IT GETS

Seven weeks after the dark day that I nearly died, I was lying on my stomach in one of the too-familiar examining rooms of the USC Medical Center. Two or three times a week, I would fight the freeway traffic from the foothills of the San Gabriel Valley to the medical campus east of the city.

Lying on the examination table, I tried not to think about the implications of the word *biopsy*. It was a challenge to keep still as the doctor struggled to scrape a specimen from my gelatinous back.

"Mr. Underwood, I know this is difficult but you must try to control the tremors."

"Why am I so cold?" I asked the doctor. "I feel like I'm freezing to death, and I can't stop shaking."

"Your condition is called exfoliative dermatitis, a severe scaling and shedding of the skin," he explained as he finished the procedure. "Your skin cells are falling off faster than your body can reproduce them. So in a way, you're freezing in the same manner a burn victim feels cold, because your skin regulates your body temperature."

"When will this end?" I complained. "I didn't know a drug reaction could last this long."

This was the same puzzle the internist who saved my life had been trying to solve for almost two months. The cycle of needles, reports, tests, drugs, therapies, and consultations with specialists offered no explanation.

"Sometimes—" the dermatologist reported as the nurse wrapped my trembling form in a warm blanket—"sometimes the onset of your continuing condition due to a drug reaction reveals an underlying malignancy."

He hesitated, trying to read my reaction.

"In your case I suspect a chronic lymphoma, most likely the leukemic variety."

The words branded my brain with searing intensity.

Malignancy. Lymphoma. Leukemia.

These were cancer words. Words for other people, not for me. Words for people who were dying, people who have no hope.

"Are you telling me that I have cancer? That I'm going to die?" I asked.

"I'm telling you," he repeated calmly, "that your symptoms indicate the possibility of an underlying malignancy. You may have an extremely serious, chronic, and potentially deadly disease."

He focused on my eyes. "But I am not saying that you are going to die. There is still a lot of medicine between you and the grave. Our first priority is to try to stabilize your skin."

WHEN THE NEWS IS AS BAD AS IT GETS

We've established how God uses the tragedies of our lives to strengthen the faith of others. But how does He care for us when the pain is ours and is overwhelming because the news is as bad as it gets?

"Your son is in jail."

"I've been unfaithful to you."

"There's been a terrible accident."

"I don't love you anymore."

"You have cancer."

In this chapter and the next, I want to help you appreciate Jesus' message of hope to those whose hearts are broken by bad news. I believe that Jesus' revolutionary reply to Martha's implication that He showed up too late will persuade you that you won't always feel the way you feel right now. It's a simple proposition—He offers us something that He wants us to accept.

Unlike you, Martha and Mary could not know how the Lord was using their difficulty to bolster the disciples' faith. They were left alone in Bethany to bury their brother with a most troubling question smoldering in their hearts. John brings the story line back west of the Jordan, to the scene of the funeral, to make sure we know that Jesus' Perean report that Lazarus had died was true (John 11:14).

> So when Jesus came, He found that he had already been in the tomb four days. (v. 17)

By the time Jesus finally showed up, Lazarus had been dead four days. Death in those days was not as sanitary as it is today—people could do little apart from anointing the body with spices to mask the smell. Jewish law did not allow the identification of a corpse after three days because the face had usually decomposed beyond the point of recognition.

Lazarus was as dead as a person could be. For four days the sisters had been numbly preoccupied with trying to make arrangements to bury their brother before his face changed. Martha supervised this period of mourning, caring for the countless details in her desperate race against the merciless decay. As the head of a prominent household, she also had to provide for the many Jews from Jerusalem who had come to comfort the sisters (vv. 18–19). She had meals to coordinate and people to put up.

And Mary? Fragile Mary was no help. She just sat there (v. 20).

But even as Martha complained to anyone who would listen that she had to do it all by herself, she secretly cherished the distraction. At least she didn't have to think about her brother's face rotting and crumbling beneath the death shroud. More important, she could ignore the questions tearing her soul apart: "Where is Jesus? Why did He let this happen? How can He say He loves us and just leave us alone like this?"

Then, without warning, phrases from the conversations among the mourners begin to penetrate the defenses of her busy mind.

Did someone say Jesus? she wonders as she looks up from her task.

"What's that?" Martha asks those standing near. "What did they say about Jesus?"

"He's here," comes the rumor. "Jesus is here … in Bethany!"

"Here, in Bethany?" Then Martha mutters through her tears, "Great. *Now* He shows up, *after* Lazarus is dead!"

Her friends try to respond. "What is that, Martha? What did you say?"

"Oh, nothing. It's nothing." She turns her face away and wipes her tears.

A sentence begins to form deep in Martha's aching heart. She has been afraid of the words, but now that Jesus is here, she can restrain them no longer.

What will she say when she sees Him and finds out that He already knows the news couldn't be worse? What would you say if you knew the news you had to report to Jesus was as bad as it gets? And worse yet, that He knew *before* the tragedy?

You Could Have Prevented This!

Leaving Mary alone in the house with her grief, Martha walked out to meet the Lord. There was no use pretending. The pain in her soul erupted in a sentence dripping with disappointment, a statement that bordered on defiance.

> "Lord, if You had been here, my brother would not have died." (John 11:21)

There, she said it. It needed to be said. It was what everyone was thinking. How could Jesus so callously let her family down? This wasn't some stranger seeking relief from a miracle worker or some critic demanding proof of His claims. This was Lazarus, Jesus' friend. And Martha and Mary, the loyal family that never failed Him when He needed a place to rest and get away.

It's impossible to know what bothered her the most as she blurted out her "if only" objection to Jesus. Maybe she was trying to be "fine" with Jesus avoiding Bethany because the authorities were after Him, but when it seemed He was willing to risk arrest *after* Lazarus had died, she realized how much this had hurt her.

Maybe Martha was hoping she would never see Jesus again so that she wouldn't have to deal with the stinging pain of His insensitivity to her family.

But there He was, walking down the road.

The One she had come to place her every hope in.

The Master who had always been so strong … and capable … and kind … and gentle.

The Teacher who always had the answers.

The Friend who had never let her down.

Until now.

If Jesus was going to cross back into hostile Judea anyway, why did He wait until it was too late?

I believe that is the thrust of the second half of her protest:

> "But even now I know that whatever You ask of God, God will give You." (John 11:22)

Martha never doubted Jesus' ability to heal the sick or prevent death. How many times had she seen it already? She knew from personal experience that God listens to Jesus.

WHAT KIND OF FRIEND WITHHOLDS HIS CARE AT THE PRECISE MOMENT YOU NEED HIM MOST?

Her doubts had to do with Jesus' *willingness to help her*, someone He had called His friend.

What kind of friend withholds

His care at the precise moment you need Him most? This was the tension throbbing in Martha's heart when Jesus finally showed up. She tried to control her emotions as she reported the worst news she'd ever had to report to the best friend she'd ever had.

"Lazarus is dead, and You could have made it better. You could have prevented this, but You refused! And my heart is broken. I thought You loved me. What a friend we have in Jesus? Right!"

What Love Is This?

I was right where Martha was the night I declared to Judy that I was through with God. Since the day the doctors gave me the worst news I'd ever heard—"It's cancer"—life had drained my eyes of tears and my heart of hope. Knowing that Jesus was watching and that His Father was aware seemed only to make it worse.

How could a Lord who professed to be my Friend and a God who claimed to be my Father allow this to go on? How could the One who claimed to be my Advocate, sitting at the right hand of the One who promised to hear my prayers, remain so insensitive to my pleadings?

I wasn't getting better; I was getting worse. My prayers sounded something like this:

> *Lord Jesus, if You had been here, this disease would not have weakened me to the point that I can't even hold my grand-babies. And it's not as if I haven't asked. I have! And don't tell me that the Father doesn't listen to You. I know He does. You could have prevented this! I don't doubt Your power; I've seen it*

too many times. I doubt Your love ... for me. This is not the way someone cares for a friend. I am not Your friend!

Father, even now I know that whatever Your beloved Son asks, You will give Him. If You wanted to give me healing, You could. In a nanosecond I would be whole. If You intervened, I could have my life back. But You won't. You won't even help a little by stopping the itching for one night's sleep, or restoring my face and hands so that I can go out in public, and my grandchildren won't cringe when I approach them. It's not that I doubt Your power. I doubt Your love ... for me. This is not the way to treat a child. I am not Your child!

Maybe you feel like this. You hate to admit it, but you are seriously questioning the Lord's love for you as His friend and the Father's care for you as His child. If you do, I want to show you why your honesty with yourself and God is not the sad end of your dealings with Him, but rather the exciting beginning to a level of intimacy known only to those who trust God enough to become totally vulnerable to Him.

YOU HATE TO ADMIT IT, BUT YOU ARE SERIOUSLY QUESTIONING THE LORD'S LOVE FOR YOU.

What might Jesus say to you or me when we admit that we doubt His devotion to us? His reply would begin in the same way He answered Martha. Jesus is no more threatened by our doubts now than He was by Martha's. Rather than defending His tardy arrival, He directs her thoughts beyond the smothering limitations of this world.

A New Reality

In a pattern that marked Jesus' care for His followers—one that would only intensify as the dark days of His death drew near—Jesus encourages Martha with an extraordinary promise to lift Lazarus up to a place where he will never feel pain, and to a time that will never end. This pledge hinges on Jesus' power, not to do the easy things Martha has been thinking about—heal the lame and sick—but to do the hard thing she has never considered—to personally guarantee that the life of His people will never end and that every one of us will be with Him in heaven.

Christ talked a lot about heaven. He didn't teach about heaven as a theologically abstract place. He described it as His home—a reality. His Father is in this place (Luke 10:21), where everything is just the way He wants it (Matt. 6:10). He encouraged His followers to invest there (vv. 19–21). He came from there (John 3:13) and longed to return. And He promised to take His followers there to live with Him (14:1–3).

Decades later, Jesus would let Paul (2 Cor. 12:1–6) and John (Rev. 4:1) peek into the wonder of His heavenly home. He didn't allow Paul to say much about it, except that it is a "far better" place (Phil. 1:23), but He instructed John to write an extended book about heaven and the events leading up to the time when He will come back from there to rule the world (Rev. 1:11).

The Bible tells us just enough about heaven to make us really want to go there, especially during the times when life down here hurts too much. All who enter and live there will be like Christ (Rom. 8:29; 1 John 3:2). It is a place of breathtaking beauty (Rev. 21:1—22:7), full of supremely interesting and stimulating citizens (Heb. 12:22–24), who constantly worship Christ (Rev. 19:3). Everyone there will experience life (2 Tim. 4:8) and an intimacy with Jesus (Rev. 22:4) unattainable here on earth. Heaven will be full of opportunities to serve Christ (Rev. 22:3) in holiness (Rev. 21:27) and glory (2 Cor. 4:17; Rev. 21:4–5).

It's quite a neighborhood Jesus is preparing for His people, wonderfully different from the streets we walk down on this globe. It is a *new reality,* where the new life He gives to us on earth can be fully expressed, released, and enjoyed.

And this hope of a new reality in heaven is where Christ tenderly turns Martha's earthbound hopelessness.

Jesus had a way of responding to His followers with exasperating surprise. Refusing to allow people to direct the dialogue, He forced the conversation toward transcendent issues. His abrupt rebuttal to Martha's not-so-subtle reminder that she was acutely aware of His God-given power to heal is one of His most dramatic "But did you ever think of this?" counterpoints in all of Scripture:

> "Your brother will rise again." (John 11:23)

We must keep this sentence within the tension of the inspired text if we want to really grasp the revolutionary weightiness of Jesus' words. Devout Jews during Jesus' time believed in the resurrection of the dead. Job, Moses, David, and the prophets had placed hope of the resurrection of the body in every spiritually minded Hebrew's heart (Job 19:25–27; Ex. 3:6; Ps. 16:8–11; Isa. 26:19; Zech. 14:5). Christ intensified His followers' expectations of entering a future kingdom (Matt. 21:31–32; John 2:19–22; 5:28–29).

So the idea of a resurrection is nothing new to Martha. She quickly—too quickly—agrees with Jesus.

> "I know that he will rise again in the resurrection at the last day." (John 11:24)

I believe this is Martha's way of letting the Lord know that she is fully aware of what He is going to say. "If You think I don't know that Lazarus will rise at the end of the age for life in the kingdom, You're wrong."

As a devout Jew, Martha had sided with the Pharisees against the Sadducees' denial of a bodily resurrection. Her declaration of faith in *a resurrection* accurately professes the teaching of the conservatives of her day with memorized detail.

I suspect that Martha's practiced precision was edged with the same aggravation we feel when someone offers some well-worn spiritual fact to our hurting hearts. "Yeah, sure. I know. Everything will work out just fine. Romans 8:28 guarantees it. Can't wait until I'm as fine as you are right now!"

"Right, right … James 1:2–3 promises that every trial is an opportunity for growth. Just think of how much patience I'm going to have when this mess is over!"

I picture Martha rolling her eyes in the same way I did when people phoned my hospital room and quoted these verses to me. It wasn't that I didn't believe what they were saying. I was just disappointed in their inability to offer something more and maybe a little wounded by what felt like tactless optimism.

If we could read Martha's mind as she mouthed the words of 11:24, I believe her thoughts were more forlorn than furious.

No, not You too! You're my Master, the One who always explained my pain with words I had never heard before. Every rabbi in town has tried to console me by reminding me of the coming resurrection. Since You decided not to heal my brother, at least tell me something new, something more hopeful. Come on, Jesus. You have to do better than that.

Jesus, who could read Martha's mind, made sure that she understood that He wasn't referring to the resurrection she had assumed He was. With startling simplicity and timing, Jesus introduces the foundational hope of Christianity.

> "Though he may die, he shall live.... Shall never die." (John 11:25–26)

Her mind tries to comprehend the words.

Did I hear what I think I heard? Did Jesus just say that there is a resurrection that is as much here and now as it is there and then?

> "Though he may die, he shall live.... Shall never die."

Martha was the first to begin thinking beyond the older images of a way-out-there resurrection. For the first time, Jesus speaks clearly of a radical resurrection the teachers never anticipated. In the years to come, His followers would understand more fully that this resurrection belongs only to His people, a new order (1 Tim. 6:16) of creation (Col. 2:9–15). But Martha had heard all she needed to begin hoping for something else. She immediately realized that Jesus was speaking of an entirely new category of life, a type of life that death could not interrupt.

I don't have to imagine the impact of those words on her heart because I remember the day they hit mine. You don't have to imagine it either. The "something else" Martha wondered at on that day can be yours today. In fact, today could be your most important day ever—a day like the day I'm about to describe to you in the next chapter. If you want to know why God might call today your most important day ever, then keep reading.

Chapter 6

MY MOST IMPORTANT DAY

The long drive home from the doctor's office on the afternoon the word *cancer* was mixed into my diagnosis is a dramatic memory blurred by tears and confusion. The closer I got to home, the more I realized I had no idea what to say to Judy. Thankfully she was still at work when I pulled into the driveway. I dedicated the time to rehearsing my report.

"I have cancer."

"They think it might be cancer, or lymphoma, a leukemia they say … something like that."

There is simply no good way to tell the person you love more than life itself that you have a deadly disease, especially if you have never thought about what you would say. I stumbled through the announcement. We held each other and cried. Then we phoned the children and tried to give them the bad news as courageously, spiritually, and selflessly as we could.

On that day of bad news, another day—the day I received the best news I would ever hear—kept me from the panicky edge of hope. The good news of that day decades earlier eclipsed the gloom of the day we reported the dark words of malignancy to our family.

It was the most important day of my life, the day the reality of Jesus' amazing sentences to Martha began to grip my heart.

> "I am the resurrection and the life. He who believes in Me, though he may die, he shall live. And whoever lives and believes in Me shall never die." (John 11:25–26)

THE JESUS MOVEMENT IN MY HEART

I will never forget that day. It was during a very surprising time—the end of the weird but wonderful sixties. For reasons of curiosity more than interest, early that evening I had tuned in to Billy Graham's Anaheim, California, crusade on television. The Jesus Movement has spilled over the coastal mountains of Southern California into the central valley. Just on the other side of those mountains was my hometown of Bakersfield—the first central valley town to feel the impact of this student-led advance of Jesus' message. From our pagan perspective, our friends were dropping like flies to these Jesus freaks. My friend Bobby was one of those we felt had "fallen" into the Jesus crowd.

The things Dr. Graham was saying about Jesus Christ that night hit me hard. Bobby had encouraged me to watch the telecast. And I had to talk to Bobby—now! Instead of calling him on the phone, I drove the six blocks to his house. The closer I came to his address, the more absurd this adventure seemed. *This is crazy. What am I going to say to Bobby? "I want to be a Jesus guy too"? I'll just drive by his house. He's probably not home anyway.*

I had talked myself out of it by the time I entered his cul-de-sac. But there was Bobby, standing in his front yard in the light of the streetlamp! He immediately recognized my hot '69 GTO. We had cruised around in it together many times before he got all religious on me.

I returned his wave, pulled next to the curb, and rolled down the window.

"Hey, Bobby."

"Hey, Eddie. Did you see Billy on TV?" he asked.

To this day I cannot recall a word from Dr. Graham's message. All I know is that whatever he said, I had to know more.

I leaned out my car window. "Bobby, I need to talk to you. I did watch Billy Graham—that's why I came here tonight. I don't know what to do. I have to talk to someone."

Bobby smiled. "I know just how you feel, Eddie. I don't know a lot, but I do know this …"

As my friend explained the core message of the good news of the gospel—the same message Jesus presented to Martha in Bethany—I knew this was the best news I would ever hear.

The sixties had been a tumultuous decade of dramatic changes, tremendous hope, and bitter disillusionment. And I was right in the middle of it. I had to admit that my life was not getting better. No matter how hard I tried to medicate the pain, my defeats and disappointments were escalating at a discouraging pace.

Guys I had grown up with were dying in Vietnam, and my

too-often duties as a pallbearer forced me to stare into eternity. Lifelong relationships were unraveling under the approaching pressures of adulthood. My friends were flawed, and so was I. We hurt one another in terrible ways. The seething anger in my gut boiled out of my life with scalding wrath toward anyone who crossed me—family, friend, or stranger.

JESUS TURNED MY WEARY SOUL'S CONCENTRATION FROM ALL THAT WAS WRONG WITH MY LIFE ON EARTH TO ALL THAT WAS WONDROUS ABOUT THE LIFE FROM HEAVEN HE WANTED TO GIVE ME.

And then, the words of Jesus …

"Though he may die, he shall live.… Shall never die."

Bobby quoted the first Bible verse my ears would ever *really* hear: "For God so loved the world that He gave His only begotten Son, that whoever believes in Him should not perish but have everlasting life" (John 3:16).

"Is He saying what I think He's saying?" I asked. Like Martha, my weary heart tried to grasp the realities of grace and mercy.

God loves me?

Jesus died for me?

Should not perish?

Everlasting life?

And just like He did with Martha, Jesus turned my weary soul's concentration from all that was wrong with my life on earth to all that was wondrous about the life from heaven He wanted to give me.

With Jesus, It's Personal

Once we begin to understand Jesus' words, an astounding awareness breaks through: *Jesus will take personal responsibility for me!* These are not religious ideas; He is making a promise.

Setting Himself apart from every spiritual teacher of all time, Jesus looks Martha in the eye and says, "I am the resurrection and the life" (John 11:25). He assures her of His ability to guarantee the eternal destiny of all who place their lives in His hands.

> "He who believes in Me, though he may die, he shall live. And whoever lives and believes in Me shall never die." (vv. 25–26)

Even if they die, He will raise them up.

Even while they live, He will give them a life that never ends.

Jesus doesn't ask us to get started making a new and better life for ourselves. He wants to give us a new life to start living. A life that is never interrupted, that goes on forever in heaven. A life that begins here on earth, right where we are. Not because we earn it, but because we *ask* for it. "Believe in Me," Jesus promised, "and I will give you everlasting life" (see John 6:47).

Even though Jesus loves us with unlimited love, He never forces His love on anyone.

Even though Jesus loves us with unlimited love, He never forces His love on anyone. Those who receive His love receive His personal guarantee.

On the most important day of my life, I received Jesus' love as my friend explained the best news I'd ever heard—that Jesus took personal responsibility for me.

On the worst day of my life, when I heard the worst news I'd ever heard, that day years ago when I received Jesus' love anchored my heart to the hope of living with Him forever in heaven.

Though the news was devastating, I knew that if the doctor's predictions of my impending death came true, Jesus would seamlessly usher me into His presence.

Though my heart was breaking over all that I might miss on earth, I knew that Judy, my children, and most of my friends shared my confidence in Jesus' personal guarantee that we will all live forever with Him in heaven.

You may be wondering how I can be so sure I have received Jesus' love—love that guarantees my forever home with Him in heaven. Maybe my confidence seems a little presumptuous, even arrogant. *How can anyone say that? How can people be so sure that Jesus will accept them?*

I can know for the same reason Jesus told Martha she could be sure that He took personal responsibility for her.

Do You Believe This?

Jesus' conversation with Martha presented some jolting claims. Standing before her in an obviously human body, He asked her to accept as factual what she could not see and what no rabbi, prophet, or king in the history of Israel had ever professed.

> "I am the resurrection and the life. He who believes in Me, though he may die, he shall live. And whoever lives and believes in Me shall never die." (John 11:25–26)

It was time for Martha to face the reality of Jesus' teaching that His Father loves people so much that He gives new life to all who believe in the Son (John 3:16; 5:24; 6:47).

His next question brings her to the decision that divides humanity: *"Do you believe this?"* (John 11:26).

"Martha, from the first time we met," Jesus says, "I have presented Myself as the long-awaited Christ, the Savior. I have always explained My reason for coming into this world as a rescue—to bring eternal life to all who believe. Now I have clearly told you what this means for you and your family. Even if you die, I will resurrect you and you will live forever. I love you so much. I want to take personal responsibility for you. I guarantee it."

Do *you* believe this?

There it is—the profoundly simple transaction that brings the hope of heaven to hurting hearts. It contains two parts—one is our responsibility, the other is His promise. If you believe this, He will be your resurrection and your life.

Martha's reply confirms her belief in Jesus.

> "Yes, Lord, I believe that You are the Christ, the Son of God, who is come into the world." (John 11:27)

Like Martha, I believe this. I believe that Jesus is the Christ—my Savior who takes personal responsibility for me. Like Martha, I believe that Jesus is the Son of God—the only One who can personally guarantee my destiny. Like Martha, I believe that Jesus came to earth for that one primary reason—to rescue me because of His and His Father's intensely proactive love for me.

And that belief, that trust in Him, makes every difference when I wake up in the middle of the night and remember that I have leukemia. Even if God's answer to my prayer to live and serve here on earth is no, I know I will continue living and serving Him forever in heaven.

This is the one prayer God never says no to. When we ask Him to give us eternal life because we believe in His Son, He *always* says yes.

YOUR MOST IMPORTANT DAY

You are reading this book because you or someone you love feels trapped in a hopeless tragedy. Jesus chose just such a moment in the life of Martha of Bethany to personalize His majestic claim to the titles *Christ* and *Son of God*.

It was the most important day of Martha's life. Jesus' primary concern for her transcended her present pain. His love pressed her for a decision to trust Him in a way that guaranteed His eternal care. She responded to His love by placing her destiny in His hands.

Could it be that Jesus is working through the heartrending condition of your life to offer you the same personal guarantee He offered to Martha that day?

I think He is.

He wants you to place your future in His hands. He wants you to know that no matter what happens next, eventually you will live with Him in heaven forever.

He wants you to believe.

The most important day in Martha's life was not the day Jesus relieved her urgent pain by raising Lazarus from the dead, but the day she stood before the Lord Jesus and believed in Him. It was the day she received the life she, her sister, and her brother have been enjoying in heaven with Jesus every day for nearly two thousand years.

The most important day in my life was not the day in the year 2000 when my internist saved my life. Neither was it the day in 2006 when my oncologist told me I could go off my cancer meds. My most important day was that day in the 1960s when I knelt down in my friend's yard and received Christ by believing in Him. That was the day Jesus took personal responsibility for me, the day that guaranteed my future forever with Him and all my redeemed loved ones and friends in heaven.

So, my friend, could today be your most important day? Jesus had you personally in mind when He died on the cross to pay for your sins.

If you've never received His gift of eternal life, make this your moment to kneel before Him with a believing heart:

Lord, I understand that You died on the cross because You love me and want to give me eternal life. I am persuaded that Your Father sent You to rescue me from my sin. I believe that You died for my sin and arose. I trust You to give me eternal life. I confess that You are the resurrection and the life and that all who believe in You will never die. ***I believe this.*** *Thank You, Father in heaven, for Your free gift of eternal life. In Jesus' name, amen.*

When you ask God for eternal life by believing in His Son—trusting in Jesus—He honors that request. You can trust Him to always grant a believing petition for new life. You'll never have to wonder about your future. When you believe in Jesus, you receive His guarantee to take you to the most special place in the universe—the personal space in heaven He is preparing for you (John 14:1–3).

THERE'S ALWAYS HEAVEN

To live with the hope of heaven is to live with a lot to be thankful for. Somehow, in the bewildering disenchantment of feeling like God has let us down on earth, we forget that He will not let us down when it comes to His promise of heaven.

I don't know why, but often those of us who have been Christians the longest find it most difficult to remember that there is always heaven. Younger believers seem more captivated by the new reality they live—Jesus' promise that He is their resurrection and life.

I'll never forget the horribly inadequate feelings I struggled with as a young pastor as I sat in a dying man's hospital room. His name was Nick. Nick and his wife had recently come to our church. I knew the moment I met them that they had never heard the good news about Jesus and that the Lord had sent them to us from a decidedly non-Christian lifestyle. In spite of their rough edges, they were open to the truth as I explained Jesus' promise of new life. It had only been a few months earlier that they had knelt in my office together trusting in Christ and expressing their belief in Him.

When we heard that Nick was critically ill, Judy and I rushed to the hospital. From the moment we walked in, it was obvious that only the respirator was keeping Nick alive. The doctor confirmed our suspicion, telling us that there was no brain activity.

"The family needs to make a decision," he said as he looked to me for help or insight.

His wife understandably protested. "He was fine yesterday. It was just a cough that got worse and worse until he panicked. He asked me to bring him here, so I did. But he was doing fine last night when I left him!"

The doctor kindly explained that the infection in Nick's lungs was extremely aggressive and resistant to antibiotics. During the night the nurse had discovered that he'd stopped breathing. They had tried to resuscitate him, but he didn't respond. Hoping they could save him, the staff put Nick on the ventilator. But the tests revealed that his brain had been without oxygen too long.

Lying before this young wife was the body of the man she had spent her entire adult life with, but there was no real life in the body. Only the machine-generated oxygen kept the cells, molecules, and organic systems functioning.

After praying with her, I asked, "What do you want to do?"

Surprisingly, she looked at me and smiled. A sudden insight had caused her to smile, and the sight of that smile amazed me. "Wait a minute," she said. "If Nick's really dead, then he's in heaven with Jesus. Isn't he?"

"That's right," I assured her. "Jesus promised to give Nick new life, eternal life, the moment he believed. And we both know that Nick believed in Jesus. We were there!"

She instructed the wide-eyed doctor to let Nick go, assuring him that her husband was already in heaven.

Judy and I held her and prayed as Nick's lifeless body failed. We joined her in praising God for our hope of heaven, which made every difference on the day her news was as bad as it gets.

I wish I could say that my long-held faith was as strong as her newly acquired belief. I wish I could say that I never doubted His love on the day the bad news came, but I can't. The temporary hurt overwhelmed my eternal hope for a time. As usual, Jesus was patient with me because He loves me and knows what it feels like to live with the pain of being human. His Spirit gently whispered in my ear, reminding me that this is not all there is. I am part of another reality. I am going to heaven because I believe in Jesus and He is worthy of my trust.

For years I have preached a sermon titled "When Life Hurts Too Much, Think About Heaven." I can tell you from personal experience how powerful this advice really is. Hardly a week goes by that some red bump on my skin or some strange twinge in my gut doesn't bring terror to my soul. When I think about heaven and pause to thank Jesus for His gift of life, I am always strengthened and refreshed.

How long has it been since you honestly thanked the Lord for His sure promise of heaven? Do you need to pause right now to "think about heaven"? If so, may I offer a transparent but thankful prayer to express your feelings to God?

Father, this hurts so much. I never thought I would have to face something like this. It's hard for me. Sometimes I feel like it's too hard and You don't even care. But this I do know. I know that Jesus will keep His promise to take me to heaven. I know that He is the resurrection and the life for me. O my Father, I do thank You for my sure hope of heaven, even when I don't understand what is happening to me on earth. Please make this hope even sweeter to me in the days ahead. I need You, Lord. I need You now. In Jesus' name, amen.

As wonderful as this hope of heaven is—secured by the most important day of our lives—it isn't the only day Jesus is interested in. There are other days He never ignores. Dark days. Desperate days.

Before you conclude that Jesus' love and care for you can only make a difference in heaven, you need to read the rest of chapter 11 of John's gospel.

In the same way Jesus' marvelous pledge to Martha invites a belief that embeds the comfort of heaven in the soul of every Christian, His next words to her ask us to believe a promise that unlocks the blessing of His care in our darkest days on earth.

Chapter 7

HEARTBREAKING INTIMACY

Do you remember Judy's prayer for me the night I concluded that I was not God's child? Refusing to agree with me, she declared her continuing faith:

"I'm not going to argue with you, Eddie. I choose to trust Him and ask God to bring you back to both of us—Him and me."

We've talked about Martha. Now, in these concluding chapters I want to tell you how God used the story of Jesus' response to Mary's anguish over Lazarus's death to answer Judy's prayer. My journey back to my Lord and my wife began when I realized the deep emotions Jesus displayed over the suffering of His friends. Then, as my heart was turning toward Him, His reminder to the sisters that belief and glory are connected provided the key insight that helped me walk through my tragedy *with* the Lord.

I believe that the picture of a grieving Jesus and the words that came from His lips can do the same for you. What God allows in your life may seem crushing. But the heavy load will be much lighter if you allow His Son to help you in the same way He helped Mary and Martha ... in the same way He helped me.

Many people, even Christians, never take their faith to this level. If you're not desperate to receive God's comfort on His terms, you should probably stop reading right now. When Jesus comforted His friends, He refused to agree to their demands. But He did react to their tears and respond to their trust. If you are ready to accept God's best care for you rather than your ideas about how He should show His concern, then this is the chapter that will take you across the threshold of *demanding* to the lasting joy of *trusting.*

> When Jesus comforted His friends, He refused to agree to their demands. But He did react to their tears and respond to their trust.

He's Calling Your Name

For some reason, we usually describe encounters with God from our point of view. We *seek* God, *find* God, *turn away* from God, or, as Judy put it in her despairing prayer for me, ask God to "bring someone back to Him."

If you look at the relationship from God's perspective, He is the Pursuer. The Old Testament is full of stories about the people of Israel trying to get away from their God. But God would not let them get away. He sent tragedies, blessings, miracles, judgments, and prophets. We may feel more comfortable thinking we are distancing ourselves from Him, but He never needs a break from us.

One of Jesus' messianic titles is the Lion of Judah (Gen. 49:8–10; Rev. 5:5). If you've ever watched a lion pursuing game, you have an accurate picture of Jesus' relentless pursuit of those He loves.

On one of our trips to Africa, our driver suddenly stopped and shouted, "Lion, lion!" We watched for over an hour as two lionesses stalked a small herd of zebra. Patiently, the lions crawled through the tall grass, drawing closer to their prey before charging for the kill. The bolting zebra avoided their claws over and over again. But the lions never gave up. Regrouping, they moved to new avenues of approach. I asked one of our colleagues who had grown up in Africa how long this would go on.

"Until they make the kill," he said.

No time limit.

No giving up.

No coming back later.

No need for a rest.

It was this same Lion of Judah who waited for Mary on the road outside of Bethany.

> And when [Martha] had said these things, she went her way and secretly called Mary her sister, saying, "The Teacher has come and is calling for you." (John 11:28)

Jesus called to Mary.

Everything we know about impetuous Martha anticipates her running back to the house, shouting, "Jesus is here, and He said our brother will live." The only explanation for her secrecy is that Jesus told her to send Mary. He wanted to speak to Mary … alone (v. 30).

"The Teacher, the incomparable speaker of truth, comfort, and love who has always explained life to us, is here. And He is calling for you."

Mary, I'm here. I never abandoned you.

Mary, it's Me. I had to come to you.

Mary, Mary, Mary. I'm calling your name.

Mary.

Mary did not come to Jesus; He came to her and called her name. When she heard He was calling, she turned to Him.

John makes sure we know that she ran to Jesus without delay. "As soon as she heard … she arose quickly" (John 11:29). Her exit from the house was so abrupt that her guests felt the need to explain her rude departure. "She is going to the tomb to weep there" (v. 31).

I WILL NEVER LEAVE YOU

As God was answering Judy's prayer to bring me back to Him (and her), I really did turn to Him. But I didn't have to "go" to Him. Jesus was always there.

FRIEND, YOU DO NOT HAVE TO "COME BACK" TO JESUS, BUT YOU DO NEED TO TURN TO HIM.

The night I decided not to pray, He was there. He said, "I will never leave you nor forsake you" (Heb. 13:5).

When I threw my Bible against the wall, He was there. And He was calling my name. "My sheep hear my voice," He said.

When my sweetheart despaired of what to do, He was calling my name.

Friend, you do not have to "come back" to Jesus, but you do need to turn to Him. He has always been there with you, and He is calling your name.

One of the main reasons I wrote this book is to help you see Jesus walking toward you with tears in His eyes, calling your name. As I write these words, my prayer for you is that you will follow Mary's lead. Turn to the waiting Teacher's arms, and ask Him "Why?"

WHY, LORD, WHY?

I have learned that intimacy with God—the nearness of our relationship with Him—is one of the most surprising variables for those who suffer. You struggle to contain your disillusionment in ways that those less committed to Christ might never encounter.

Notice the dramatic difference between Martha and Mary when they saw Jesus for the first time after Lazarus's death.

> When Mary came where Jesus was, and saw Him, she fell down at His feet, saying to Him, "Lord, if You had been here, my brother would not have died." (John 11:32)

The words are identical, but the behavior could not be more divergent. Martha's story reads more like an interview. Mary loses control as she falls at Jesus' feet weeping (v. 33).

I'm sure some of this response was temperament, but I think a lot of it had to do with Mary's nearness to Christ. Mary was Jesus' especially devoted follower and friend.

Mary had already demonstrated that she cared more about being near Jesus than her reputation as a hospitable Jewish woman (Luke 10:38–42). In a few days, Mary would wash Jesus' feet with expensive perfume—a lavish display of worship and devotion. In those days a woman's contribution to her future husband was preserved in this way. She wasn't just emptying a bottle of her favorite fragrance; she was offering all her family had been saving as her dowry. Judas, the betraying and greedy disciple, would rebuke her for "wasting" a year's wages in one impulsive act of worship (John 12:1–7). Her need to be near Jesus was greater than her concern for her reputation as a prudent Jewish woman.

It wasn't simply emotional Mary being more demonstrative than sensible Martha. Mary lost control because her heart was more broken than Martha's. Mary was closer to Jesus than Martha was.

The underlying principle of disillusionment is this: *The deeper the relationship, the deeper the hurt.*

Over the past seven years, I've talked with hundreds of Mary-like followers of Christ who, like me, were taken aback by their emotions when they felt like Jesus didn't care.

- The father whose life was wholly dedicated to God and his family was called to the emergency room because his daughter had been beaten almost to death by her promiscuous husband, whom she had met at a prestigious Christian university. When it all came out, he raged in my office. "I committed her to God the day she was born! We never missed church. I taught her the Bible. I've prayed for her every day for thirty-six years. I didn't raise her for this. Why, Lord, why?"

- The pastor who had poured his life into a church and was told during his sabbatical that the board had decided to let him go. He paced the floor of his home like a caged bear, crying out to me, "Ed, what more could I have done? Sure, I've made mistakes, but there has never been one day I didn't give God everything I have for these people. What do You want from me, Jesus? Why, Lord, why?"

- The couple that dedicated their retirement to a small community, only to be hurt terribly by one church after another. Just when it seemed they were finally settling into a life that was making a difference, she became ill. Instead of serving others in the name of Christ, they spent their days driving to and from medical facilities. "I can't understand why the Lord won't release us to help these hurting people. No one cares for them but us, and there is little we can do unless her health improves. This doesn't make any sense for us, for this town, or for the kingdom. Why, Lord, why?"

Before you judge these dear friends as unspiritual or weak, notice what they have in common with Mary: Their relationship with the

Lord was so deep they could not keep it in. They got it out. They fell at His feet and asked Him "Why?" They were honest with God.

MAD AT YOU TONIGHT!

A few months after the evening I first turned my back on the Lord, I was deep into the battle with what I now know was lymphoma, and I tried to turn away from God again. My journal entry from June 2000 reads, "Father, yesterday I melted down in rebellious resignation. 'Okay, whatever, Lord … have Your way. I'm tired of trying to pray.' My sin was that I distanced myself from You. Forgive me, Lord."

The day I spoke of in my journal was the second time I had decided not to pray.

I was taking eighty milligrams of steroids a day and running to the doctor two to three times a week, but nothing—and I mean nothing—relieved the chaos of my skin.

I thought I had already experienced the worst of my illness, that my inability to pray or lack of interest in prayer was a temporary setback. After all, it had been ten weeks since my knee had been infected. I had endured several weeks in the hospital when I almost died, and then several weeks of a hellish rash. One moment of weakness before God the night my grandchildren visited after Disneyland was to be expected, wasn't it? I thought I could move on from this moment and things would get better.

I was wrong!

A few days after I was diagnosed with lymphoma, we traveled to Colorado to do a wedding for a dear friend. Judy told me we should stay home, that I wasn't up to it. When we returned to Los Angeles, new sores developed on top of the sores that were already on my back and abdomen.

"What is this?" I asked my oncologist.

"I'm so sorry, Ed," she said. "You have shingles. Your immune system is so weak; you're having a difficult time fighting off any bug. This is a virus that has lived in your body since you had chicken pox, waiting for opportunity. We'll try to manage the pain, but actually this is quite common when someone has been as critical as you for so long."

Lymphoma, incurable rash, critically aggressive exfoliation, kidney failure, liver failure, and now *shingles*?

It's a unique pain, shingles. It feels like worms are crawling just beneath the surface of your skin. Even the weight of the bedsheet is unbearable. You cannot ignore it.

The entire way home from USC's Norris Cancer Center, I kept it together. "I can do this, Lord. I mean, *we* can do this, Lord. One day at a time. I know a lot of people who have survived shingles. Help me," I kept repeating as the worms crawled under my scorched and flaking skin.

Then when I got home, Judy greeted me with wonderful news: "Something is wrong with our air conditioner."

Southern California in late June and no air conditioning. One hundred and five degrees in the house, and the doctor had told me to "stay out of the heat."

That did it.

When Judy asked me what we should do, I told her honestly, "I don't know. We're tapped out. Just paying the deductibles from all of these surgeries, hospital stays, and medications has stripped us of every penny and maxed out our credit cards. I guess we just ... suffer alone."

When the blazing California sun slipped mercifully beyond the horizon to the west of us, we went to bed.

Judy turned to me. "Well, honey, let's pray before we try to go to sleep."

"I'm not praying anymore. Not tonight anyway. If you want to pray, pray!" I turned my back to her.

This time, instead of arguing Judy turned to her side. "Okay, God, we're not praying tonight. We're mad at You," she said.

And she was right.

MESSY HONESTY

Since then I have wondered at the drama of that night, the night Judy and I surprised ourselves with a common animosity toward God. What was going on in our hearts? Were we demonstrating some weakness of faith that should disqualify us as spiritual leaders? Was it simply a childlike response to the momentary but spiking sting of our desperate circumstances? Or was this a crisis of faith we had to face, a process the Lord uses to test the faith of His people?

There are times when I feel like I could answer yes to each of these possibilities. But as I look back at that evening, with the critical mass of insight these years have rendered to my heart, I feel it was a time when Judy and I broke through a spiritual threshold vital to our personal experience of faith.

Never forget that the statement "Christianity is about relationship with Christ" describes the central dynamic of our faith. Like any relationship, our relationship with God is bound to hit peaks and valleys. The primary difference is the biblical knowledge that any disagreement with Him puts us on the wrong side of truth. Still, like any intimate personal connection—husband and wife, siblings, lifelong friends, or partners in business or ministry—strains and troubles are inevitable.

Especially when we are close to God. When we are more like Mary than like Martha.

Those who study interpersonal health tell us that the worst option when facing confusion or conflict is to ignore these issues, hoping they will go away. People who try to deny the tension settle into a depressing codependent dance that hinders or even precludes true intimacy. The most satisfying and sustaining marriages, friendships, partnerships, and families are those that honestly address their differences and in the process of working through the pain move to ever-deepening levels of closeness.

Judy and I did not deny our anger at God. Of course, we ultimately worked our way through it. The next day we were seeking our way back to that "trust His love" way of life that had been ours. What we did not do was settle for a less-than-authentic canned answer to the doubts of believers that would have doomed us to the penitentiary of plastic Christianity.

Friends, intimacy is messy. Always has been, always will be.

There are simply times when the mess of this world and the mess of our flesh upend the sanitized versions of Christianity that too many denying believers face life with. That kind of Christianity only works when the categories of our life stay within the concrete levees of our anticipated control systems. When the hundred-year rain comes or the class-five hurricane hits, we can only sit on the rooftop of our once-safe home wondering what went wrong.

When we look at the black holes in our lives and say, "Okay, Lord. This scares the living spit out of me, but I'm not walking around it. I'm grabbing Your hand and jumping in. If I hit some dangerous rocky bottom with a splat, so be it. I'm tired of playing like these things don't happen or matter. Something deep in my heart tells me this is necessary."

I believe this is what Judy and I did that night we refused to live in a way that sounds good in a sermon but isn't true of us. The night we refused to be subdued and safe. As in other relationships, the white water of that evening took us to a fork in the river we never even knew existed. Swept along by our emotional response to the horror of our lives, we looked up to see something—no, *feel* something—we had never felt before.

We fell at His feet and asked, "Why?"

Years later, just seven months before I finished this book, the rash returned in all its fierceness. But this time around, I have found no anger in my heart toward my heavenly Father. What I feel this time is a profound sadness. My personal pain is just one minuscule measurement of the crushing weight of the consequences of sin in this world.

A few nights ago, Judy asked me if I was mad again.

"No, honey," I told her. "I'm past that now. But I am sad. So sad that our rebellion against such a good God has brought this type of pain into the world. When I think of the hurting people in our church, pitiful people we've seen around the globe on missions trips, the pain our children and grandchildren cannot possibly escape in this life, it just makes me cry."

And I did. And I do.

As I think of some of you reading this right now, of the particular way sin has touched your life through disease, death, abandonment, and tragedy … I cry.

My sense is that if Judy and I had stuffed our anger toward God on that desperate night, these tears would not be flowing right now.

Friends, I don't know what it is in your most personal feelings toward God that scares you. I do know that the worst choice you can make is to deny those emotions and leave them brooding in your gut.

God is huge; He can take it.

Fall at Jesus' feet and ask, "Why?"

Pour out the naked reality of your innermost being to Him. He will tenderly and perfectly respond to your cry in ways that will teach you some of the most significant insights into what it means to be His child.

Like Mary, run to Jesus … fall at His feet … weep … and tell Him how you feel.

> "Lord, if You had been here, my brother would not have died." (John 11:32)

"Lord, I thought we were close. How could You let this happen? Where have You been? You have broken my heart."

"Why? Why? Why?"

If the Martha in you is still trying to keep the Mary in you from rushing to Jesus with emotional abandon, let me encourage you to let your feelings go. Your tears move God's heart. Look at what Mary's grief did to Jesus.

TEARFUL RAGE

The principle that tells us why devoted followers of Christ can't ignore or explain away the pain of feeling ignored by God works both ways: *The deeper the relationship, the deeper the hurt.*

The depth of Jesus' friendship with Mary brought on a display of emotion so profound that many Christians feel a need to explain it away. Uncomfortable with John's vivid description of Jesus' emotions, they ascribe cosmic theological motives to the Son of God.

I have a better explanation. The same explanation offered by those who were there that day: "See how He loved [Lazarus]!" (John 11:36). Jesus could not hide His feelings when He saw the pain this family He loved was enduring.

> Therefore, when Jesus saw [Mary] weeping, and the Jews who came with her weeping, He groaned in the spirit and was troubled. (v. 33)

John's choice of those two words, *groaned* and *troubled*, paints a picture of an extremely distraught Jesus. The rare word translated *groan* originally described the snorting sound of agitated horses or the grunt of a protective mother bear. When used to portray human behavior, it indicates a loud, inarticulate noise expressing angry feelings. The term *troubled* indicates an observable shuddering of the body brought on by mental or spiritual protest or anguish.

Somewhere in the mystery of God wrapping Himself in human skin, Jesus, the God-man, expressed His godly anger against the pain of sin and death through intense human emotions. Jesus could not and did not suppress His rage against the impact of all that is wrong with life.

I imagine a somewhat astonished crowd silently wondering what Jesus' expressive reaction to Mary's grief could mean. I see Him scanning the faces with a resolve that frightened them, His gaze finally stopping at the two sisters. "And He said, 'Where have you laid him?'" (v. 34).

Somewhat shaken by their Lord's conduct, the sisters quickly reply, "Lord, come and see" (v. 34).

And then something happens to Jesus that every suffering heart reading these words immediately recognizes—His anger turns to tears. "Jesus wept" (v. 35).

Using a verb found only here in the entire New Testament, John contrasts the loud wailing of the mourners (vv. 31–33) to Jesus' quiet tears. Suddenly, the Son of God begins to weep—just like His people do when rage empties their hearts of anger, leaving only grief.

I've already told you of the countless nights I groaned inarticulate, guttural screams against the rash, the weakness, the itching, the pain, the fear, the diagnosis, the unfairness, the loss. Then, weary beyond strength, I would cry myself to sleep.

I can still remember how important this picture of Jesus' anger and tears was to me during those long grievous nights. I didn't have to hide my emotions or shame myself. "You know just how this feels," I would repeat to Jesus. "Thank You for showing Your anger and Your tears at Lazarus's grave."

It's interesting that the shortest verse in the Bible—"Jesus wept"—introduces the longest debate in history about God: *If He loves me, why doesn't He do something?*

> Then the Jews said, "See how He loved him!" And some of them said, "Could not this Man, who opened the eyes of the blind, also have kept this man from dying?" (John 11: 36–37)

I wish I could come to your side right now to help you with your personal grief. I hope you'll listen to these words, because I'm going to tell you what I would say if I was sitting next to you right now: "Go ahead, scream at the pain, shed your tears, and ask your questions. But do it in the presence of Jesus, because He knows exactly how you feel."

Not intellectually, but viscerally.

No one hates your pain more than Jesus.

No one hurts for you more than Jesus.

Jesus, God-in-the-flesh, raged at the tears of His friends and wept at their graveside.

God felt grief as a man … all of it.

One thing I know: God is not trifling with you. I can't tell you that He will fix this, but I can tell you that He hates it and that it breaks His heart.

As the reality of death confronted Jesus at the tomb of Lazarus, He groaned again (v. 38). The thought of His friend's decomposing body and disappearing face on the other side of that stone sealing the cave troubled Him. The sound of Mary's cries and the sight of her tears moved Him.

Just as your cries and tears move Him.

Friend, Jesus isn't ignoring your pain; He's feeling it. He's not ashamed of your tears; He's weeping with you. The only thing that can disconnect you from His compassionate care is you. If you allow the questions nobody can answer to drive you from His presence, you will never hear the promise only He can make.

Friend, Jesus isn't ignoring your pain; He's feeling it. He's not ashamed of your tears; He's weeping with you.

I beg you to look into His tearstained face and ask Him, "Lord, my heart is broken and so is Yours—what can You promise me now?" You may feel as if the grief is too great even to think of a prayer—you simply can't find the words. Let me help you. Here are some of my words—feel free to use them if they express your heart:

Lord Jesus, I'm using Ed's words because mine won't come right now. This hurts so much that only the picture of Your tear-stained face gives me hope. Is there a promise from Your heart to mine, just for me and my broken heart? I want to hear it. I want to believe it. Give me the strength to read on and the faith to believe Your special promise for me.

His answer comes in the next few verses of John 11 and the final paragraphs of this book.

Chapter 8

GLORY IN BETHANY

The drama of our story intensifies when Jesus stands outside the cave containing Lazarus's body. Nobody speaks as Jesus wipes the tears from His face and collects Himself. I can almost hear the gasp of the small crowd gathered there when Jesus says, "Take away the stone" (John 11:39).

This was a radical command. The next time you go to a funeral, think what would happen if someone said, "Open the casket, and dump the body on the floor!"

Your disgust with that request would not compare to the revulsion these Judean Hebrews would have felt that day. The Law clearly taught that any contact with a dead body defiles. That's why they sealed the tomb with a big rock!

Martha can't accept Jesus' command and strongly protests.

> "Lord, by this time there is a stench, for he has been dead four days." (John 11:39)

The original text is even stronger: "He's a fourth-day man!"

"You can't be serious, Lord," Martha says. "The rabbis expressly forbid this. I've worked myself to exhaustion getting him in the grave so no one would have to look at his decomposed face or smell his decaying flesh. This is all wrong!"

This is a pattern Jesus rarely diverts from in a crisis: His followers can't wait for Him to show up. When He finally does, we're initially comforted by His presence. But then when He speaks, He tells us to do something that just doesn't add up.

"Take away the stone."

IF YOU BELIEVE

Jesus' radical words to me came from one of my favorite verses in the Bible, Ephesians 2:10. Most Christians know the verses immediately preceding this one. Ephesians 2:8–9 assures us that salvation from sin is a gift of God's grace to all who believe: "For by grace you have been saved through faith, and that not of yourselves; it is the gift of God, not of works, lest anyone should boast."

Verse 10 tells us why God saved us by grace through faith—to accomplish works He prepared for us in eternity past: "For we are His workmanship, created in Christ Jesus for good works, which God prepared beforehand that we should walk in them."

My command to "take away the stone" came from this verse. His Spirit let me know that He expected me to apply this verse to my life immediately.

"Ed, you're telling people everywhere to ask Me to allow you to live and serve. I want you to begin living as if it's true!"

"When, Lord?" I asked.

"Right now. Today. Serve Me today and every day I give you life … no matter what."

Oh, how I protested.

"Lord, I'm a bloated, hideous lymphoma man. No one wants to look at me. No one wants to listen to what I have to say. I'm swollen and ugly. I smell like medicine. My skin is falling off. I can't even wear church clothes. This is all wrong!"

Suddenly, at this precise moment, Jesus' promise to Martha made more sense than my objections and became the foundational truth His Spirit used to heal my broken heart.

> Jesus said to her, "Did I not say to you that if you would believe you would see the glory of God?" (John 11:40)

The thought of everyone seeing and smelling the horror of her brother's death caused Martha to forget her last conversation with the Lord. He reminds her of what she said she believed earlier, "Your brother shall rise again." And then the promise: "If you would believe you will see the glory of God."

There it is, the promise from the weeping Jesus to the broken hearts of His people.

THE PROMISE BEGINS WITH OUR RESPONSIBILITY— WE MUST BELIEVE HIM. EVEN WHEN WHAT HE SAYS SEEMS TOO ABSURD OR TOO HARD.

The promise begins with our responsibility—we must believe Him. Even when what He says seems too absurd or too hard. Martha needed to trust Jesus enough to give her permission as head of the household to take away the stone. "But, Lord, he's a fourth-day man!" I needed to trust Jesus enough to begin living as a man who still had Ephesians 2:10 works to do. "But, Lord, I'm a repulsive lymphoma man!"

That was my protest on the Sunday morning I got ready to preach my first sermon back in the pulpit at Church of the Open Door after I had been diagnosed. Judy had to dress me because my swollen fingers did not work well enough to button my own buttons. The only clothes I could tolerate were the loose-fitting garments we had bought at a local skateboarding shop.

I sat on the bed in front of the mirror weeping uncontrollably. "Look at me!" I said to Judy. Every inch of me that the clothes couldn't hide was hideous. My face, hands, and feet were swollen and my skin was a shocking hue of what I can only describe as nuclear crimson. "I look like a red monster who lost his skateboard. I can't even turn the pages of my Bible. What will visitors think? I can't keep from crying. I can't remember my sermon. I can't do this!"

The same Judy who had refused to agree with my conclusion that I wasn't God's child and begged God to bring me back to Him and to her, sat down, held my hot hands, looked into my eyes, and said, "Honey, I know this is hard. But you have to do this. You have to believe what Jesus says."

And I knew what He was asking me to believe—that this day, my Ephesians 2:10 work was to preach my first sermon as the lymphoma pastor.

I had to believe. That was my responsibility. And if I believed, He promised to fulfill His responsibility—to show me the glory of God.

You Will See

As Tom Townsend led the worship service that morning, I claimed Jesus' promise to the brokenhearted over and over again. I repeated it at least a hundred times in twenty minutes.

"If I believe, You will show me the glory of God."

"If I trust You enough to stand in that pulpit and preach today, You will somehow glorify Your Father through this feeble, cancer-worn body and these disjointed, steroid-confused words."

Martha believed Jesus, granted permission, and had the stone removed.

Jesus lifted His eyes to heaven and prayed to His heavenly Father. His rare public prayer focused everyone's attention on what He was about to do as a demonstration of God's glory that proved Jesus' claim to have come from heaven as God's only Son.

> Then they took away the stone from the place where the dead man was lying. And Jesus lifted up His eyes and said, "Father, I thank You that You have heard Me. And I know that You always hear Me, but because of the people who are standing by I said this, that they may believe that You sent Me."
>
> Now when He had said these things, He cried with a loud voice,
>
> "Lazarus, come forth!"
>
> And he who had died came out bound hand and foot with graveclothes, and his face was wrapped with a cloth. Jesus said to them, "Loose him, and let him go." (John 11:41–44)

The glory of God was so radiant at that graveside that no one could deny the cause—Jesus' prayer to His Father and His authoritative shout, "Lazarus, come forth!" The glory of God shone so brightly that Martha could not miss the connection between that glorifying call and her believing assent to take away the stone.

That morning, I walked up to the pulpit of Church of the Open Door repeating the promise: *If you believe, you will see....* I looked out over the crowd, this dear family I had missed so intensely for so many months. I knew it was hard for them to see me like this. I could see it in their eyes.

If you believe, you will see ...

My voice came out weakly. "Hi. For those who are new to our church, my name is Ed Underwood, and I am still pastor of Church of the Open Door."

If you believe, you will see ...

The congregation spontaneously jumped to their feet, clapping. Many cheered; some shouted words of blessing and encouragement. It was so unlike us to be so demonstrative!

I cried. They cried. We wiped our tears and cried again. I stumbled through Psalm 91, and we cried some more.

It may have been the best Sunday of my life.

If you believe, you will see ... You will see the glory of God.

What I didn't know then was that when God finally brought us back together, we were not the same. We were better—much better.

The Glory of God

I have a photo on my desk that never fails to put my disease in perspective. I'm standing before the congregation a few weeks before I got sick, the picture of health, lifting up a platter overflowing with grapes, looking to heaven and praying to God.

That Sunday I was wrapping up a vision series titled "From Survival to Significance." To let the people know that I was tired of our preoccupation with simple survival after a decade of turbulence and frustration, I turned to John 15 and begged God to do whatever He needed to do to give us a life of true, eternal significance.

Lord, I want my life to count forever. I don't want to be used by You to produce just a little amount of fruit. I want to see You do great things through my life and through the lives of these friends.

The questions in my mind during the weeks I was teaching that series centered on our need for healing and change.

Church of the Open Door had been devastated by years of disappointment and discord. The moral failure of a beloved pastor and a prolonged battle between the leaders and his replacement had reduced this great and historic church to a shell of her former self.

How can we ever heal and move on to living expectantly when there are so many unresolved hurts and conflicts?

Judy and I were trying to rebound from our own loss of a ministry we cherished. The wounds were still so fresh that we struggled with giving our hearts to this church.

How can we do this when the pain of all we lost before keeps us from trusting and dreaming again?

The answer to my cry for significance and to these troubling questions came in God's gift of cancer. The church that had been devastated by years of disappointment, discord, and disagreement was now one. And our unity has only grown deeper.

Recently in our small group we were reviewing the all-church prayers we ask our people to pray daily. At the top of the list was this request: "Please make us one." A lady who was relatively new to our church family remarked, "Why do you keep asking for this? I've been in church all my life, and I've never been around a group of Christians who were more unified. I think you should change this prayer from 'Make us one' to 'Keep us one.'"

THE ANSWER TO MY CRY FOR SIGNIFICANCE AND TO THESE TROUBLING QUESTIONS CAME IN GOD'S GIFT OF CANCER.

As the rest of the group agreed and some of our veteran leaders in the group paused to thank the Lord for the remarkable harmony we enjoy, I was thanking Him for my disease and His faithfulness to Jesus' promise: "You will see the glory of God."

The pastor who had always longed to be more tender and caring was crying and praying with people after services. The heart I used to hold close so that no one would bruise it is now risked openly in the name of Jesus.

Recently, a couple asked to talk with me near the end of a week I spent ministering at a family conference. They were trying to explain why the week meant so much to them, and both of them were crying. "We have never felt a pastor's heart like we feel yours. You speak the truth in ways that make us want to do what God says. You're just so loving, so gentle, so warm."

As I thanked them for their kind words of encouragement, I was admitting to the Lord that I never heard my impact on others described in this way before cancer. And I thought about Jesus' promise again:

"If you believe, you will see the *glory* of God."

A Promise of Glory

It's important for you to carefully note what I was thanking God for—the way He has used my disease to reveal *His glory.* I will be happy, overjoyed, to thank Him for the glory of healing if He ever answers that prayer with a yes. So far His answer to that request is no.

There is a difference between God saying yes to your prayer for your specific need and saying yes to your prayer to show you His glory. We can be assured that our belief in Jesus' promise means we will someday understand how God used our pain to glorify Himself. But Jesus doesn't say that God never says no to our prayers, yours or mine.

Every time someone says, "Ed, you are God's perfect choice to write this book," my first thought is *Not really.*

I have a friend in heaven named Jon Campbell who would have done a much better job. He suffered longer, believed more strongly, and encouraged more effectively than I could ever hope to.

I knew Jon as a friend and partner in ministry, the president of the company that served and represented our radio ministry. I was familiar with Jon's integrity, vision, and skill in leading Ambassador Advertising, a premier Christian media firm. We had laughed together, strategized together, dreamed together, and prayed together.

What I didn't know about Jon was what he told me the day he cleared his busy schedule to come to my side when he heard I had leukemia. He walked into my office, sat down, looked me in the eye, and said, "You probably don't know that I have lived with lymphoma for many years."

As Jon shared his personal journey through years of suffering, hope, and even disappointment, his courageous faith in God's care encouraged me. He had never mentioned it before because it had been years since he had struggled with the severest symptoms. I knew that he understood what I was going through. My distended figure and desperate scratching and the dead skin littering my office didn't distract him. Jon looked right into my broken heart and spoke kind, tender, and encouraging words.

He prayed for me that day and I prayed for him. He asked God to restore me to life and ministry; I asked God to maintain Jon's vibrant energy and that his cancer would not return.

It became obvious a few years later that God was saying yes to Jon's prayer for me, but no to my prayer for Jon.

Judy and I were privileged to pray with Jon and his dear wife, Peggy, on the last weekend of his life. I drove from his house trying not to believe that God was saying no to my prayer for my friend's life. I still struggle with God's no. In my mind it isn't fair. If ever there was a man who deserved to live, who needed to live for the sake of the gospel, it was Jon. If ever there was a Christian couple dedicated to the Lord Jesus, it was Jon and his bride.

I'm typing these words from Jon and Peggy's beachfront getaway, which Jon never really got to enjoy. It just doesn't seem right that Jon won't look out this window with his beloved Peg at his side, that she has to move forward pursuing their dreams for Christian broadcasting alone.

All I can do is cling to the Lord's promise—that He will reveal His glory in this. The promise is very specific: *If we believe, we will see His glory*. God said no to our prayers for Jon's life, but He has not said no and will not say no to our claim to His glory. He can't say no to what He has promised because He cannot lie (Titus 1:2).

Jon often talked about the "joy in the journey." The idea that you may not be able to change your circumstances, but you can change your attitude about them. This way of thinking glorifies God, and that is exactly what Jesus is trying to say to us in John 11.

So that's what I'm trying to do. Those of us who loved Jon cannot change the circumstances—he is in heaven with Jesus. But we can change our attitude about his departure—Jesus will bring glory to the Father through this.

Some of that glory is in Jon's words to the grieving loved ones of a friend who had died not long before Jon himself left this world: "I rest in the fact that our God does everything perfectly, even when our earthly view limits our understanding."

My prayer for those of you who are dealing with God's answer to your own desperate questions is that my friend's faith will help you live with the no in the same way that it is helping me. That you will be able to see God's glory no matter what His answer to your prayers might be.

Keep on praying as you rest in the fact that He does everything perfectly.

Keep on believing as you remember that your earthly view limits your understanding but doesn't limit His glory.

AN INVITATION TO GLORY

I wonder if you have made the connection yet between your personal and specific need to believe and the glory God will bring from your broken heart.

For Martha, it was trusting Jesus enough to let them take away the stone.

For our dear friend Peggy Campbell, it is trusting Jesus enough to move on without the love of her life, her courageous Jon.

For me, it is trusting Jesus enough to serve Him amid the weakness of a chronic disease.

I don't know what it is for you because I don't know what is breaking your heart.

Maybe He's asking you to believe that your marriage still has hope … after the betrayal.

> I HAVE NO IDEA HOW YOU WILL SEE GOD'S GLORY. I ONLY KNOW THAT IF YOU BELIEVE, YOU WILL SEE IT.

Maybe He's asking you to believe that He can still use you … after the failure.

Maybe He's asking you to believe that you can still go to church … after you've been hurt.

Maybe He's asking you to believe that He is still speaking to your child … after she ran away.

Or maybe He's asking you to believe what I believe—that every day is still a day to serve Him … after the diagnosis.

With every word I have written in this book I have begged God that you would listen to what His Son is saying to your broken heart: "If you believe, you will see the glory of God."

As you read these words, Jesus sits at the right hand of the Father in heaven. With tears in His eyes He whispers in His Father's ear, "This is hard for him. This breaks her heart."

In the same way I can't know what He's asking you to believe, I have no idea how you will see God's glory. I only know that if you believe, you will see it. I hope you will trust Him enough to pray this simple prayer of the brokenhearted:

Lord Jesus, I have heard You calling my name and know that You care for me. Please use my tragedy to bring glory to Your name, to bring glory to the Father. If You will tell me what it is You want me to believe, I will. I claim Your promise to my broken heart, "If you believe, you will see the glory of God."

Friend, don't let your broken heart define your life. God has so much more for you. Every tomorrow can be a day of glory … if you believe.

AFTERWORD

In the week I was putting the final touches on this book, I sent or read portions of it to several people who asked if I could give them any encouragement from God. One of the leaders at our church had received news that he had a terribly debilitating disease that no one survives. A devoted wife and mother had discovered that her Christian husband had a secret life. Another young family sat in a hospital begging God to help Daddy wake up after the trauma of a traffic accident.

As I talked with these people about the same ideas I have shared with you, I saw the power of these truths in their lives. If this book has helped you better face your days of suffering, trusting God to release all the good He means to accomplish through your pain, please write me. I would love to hear your story.

I know that living with hope in your heart through troubled times is not easy. Some days I want to give up. Nights when getting up the next day to look for God's glory seems too hard. Especially for those of us who are living with God's firm no to a desperate request.

You asked God to let your baby live, but He is asking you to move on with only her memory and the hope of seeing her in heaven. You asked Him to save your marriage, but He is asking you to raise your children as a single mom. You asked Him to let your loved one live, just as Judy asked for more time with me. But He is asking you to live out your years without the one you told Him you could not live without.

I don't know all of the pain of your personal life, but I do know some of it.

We continue to ask God to heal me of this disease, but He has continued to ask me to live each day for Him in spite of this ailment.

My skin will probably never be the same. The rashes, itching, and scaling continue daily, though thankfully none of it is severe unless the disease flares. Every three weeks, one of the nurses in our church sticks a long needle into my arm to inject medication that gives me the stamina to live an almost normal life.

The routine of my life still involves many, many trips to various doctors and specialists, and the medical bills still stretch our budget terribly.

I haven't smelled anything for four years, and probably never will again.

Hardly a week goes by that some new sore doesn't worry me to distraction: *Is it coming back? Am I going back into a three-month cancer skin peel?* Or worse, a twinge of pain in my abdomen or a sore spot around a lymph gland: *Is this it, Lord? Has the disease escaped to a vital organ?*

This is what I know my life will look like if God continues to say no to my plea for healing. But I keep coming back to the central truth that has defined my life: *"Jesus loves me! This I know, for the Bible tells me so."*

HIS LOVE FOR YOU CAN DEFINE YOUR LIFE, EVEN WHEN YOUR HEART IS BROKEN.

I wrote this book to help you see how His love for you can define your life, even when your heart is broken. You may not recover from this disease. Your husband or wife may never come back. You will never get over the death of your child. Life will always seem empty as you live on without your life partner.

Life won't quit hurting, but neither will Jesus quit caring. If you will trust Him, He will show you His glory.

You've read a lot about the ways Jesus has shown His glory to me and other sufferers I've met while He was forming the words of this book in my soul.

What about your story?

You are reading these final sentences because your broken heart believes that God will show you His glory. I want to help you as much as I can. Please visit me at my Web site, www.EdUnderwood.com, and tell me about your story. I promise to read your note and pray for you. With your permission, I may be able to use your story to encourage other fellow sufferers.

May the Lord use this book to convince you that some of your very best days are still ahead. Days filled with meaning and significance, as you become one of those uncommon people who allow Him to use your hurt to help and encourage others. And that is a glory worth living for.

Part II

The Dark Road to Glory

It's been seven years now since I got sick, and as I write these words, I am more convinced than ever of the power of the one-sentence prayer of those who would honestly admit that God has broken their heart: "Lord, I believe; show me Your glory."

People have asked me if I would give up all that the Lord has done through my disease if He would take it from me.

Most of the time the answer to that question is no. But just a few months ago, when my skin flared up again and the itchy mess replayed, I have to admit that I wished someone else could write this book.

I hope you're not disappointed in me.

I know the Lord isn't because He is favoring me by letting me be part of your life.

I also hope you're not too impressed with me.

One of my deepest fears in writing this book is that you would feel like it's for super-spiritual people who don't struggle with their faith in the same way you do. Nothing could be further from the truth.

There's no super-spiritual faith; there's just faith.

The only super part of my faith is the One I believe in. His name is Jesus Christ.

The short segments you are about to read are from my most personal records—my journal and e-mails I sent to loved ones and close friends. I've tried to arrange them in a manner that will help you in specific ways as you are trusting God to bring glory from your broken heart.

I pray that as you read my most intimate reflections you will feel God's grip on your life in a way that will carry you through your troubled times.

YOU ARE ALIVE TODAY!

When I hear that someone has just received devastating news like a bad diagnosis, a runaway child, a wayward spouse, or the death of a loved one, this is the letter I send them. This specific letter is the one I sent to our friend Joni Burchett. The same woman I told you of earlier who lost her little girl was recently diagnosed with breast cancer.

Dear Joni,

I don't know if I told you, but they took me off the cancer meds after six years! Our prayer has been *Please let Ed live and serve*. Now it has changed to *Please let Ed live and serve without the meds.*

I say this to encourage you. The daily struggle of this makes it so hard to see past the weakness and the disappointment. Here is a sentence the Lord gave me when I was fighting for one more day of life: *I am as alive today as anyone.* He helped me realize that until I take my last breath, He still has plans for me (Eph. 2:10), and that I could not conclude that this was it. So I got up and asked Him for strength for the next minute, sometimes for every minute for the next couple of days. Then for the next hour, the next day, the next week …

Sure enough—at last count, seven men I know pretty well, about my age, guys I fought fire with, men I served with in ministry, a few who stood at my bedside with panic in their eyes, or who talked on the phone with compassion and pity in their voices—are dead. Think of it, friend. People who are praying for you now are only as alive as you. It is not the meds or the docs; it is the Lord who determines when death comes to His children and the quality of their life.

I knew the Lord wanted me to do two things: Pray for healing, which I still do, and find the best doctors and do what they say, which I also still do … mostly.

So, our dear friend, know that our prayers are prayers of faith and boldness. We're not mealy mouthing the evangelical jive, "Only Your will be done." Of course His will is going to be done—He's God! He loves you; He loves us. He cares more than we can know, and *He answers prayer.* So we're going to pray our heart: *Let Joni live to see her grandchildren grow up, and please give her relief.*

But remember this: Every day you wake up, you are as alive on that day as any person on earth.

And every day you are alive is a day the Lord Jesus has something for you to do. It may be to survive your chemo treatment. It may be to sleep and pray. But there is a reason He gave you breath.

Never forget that every day you wake up is another day that the Lord is giving you hope that there will be more.

Like every Christian who has ever faced a tragedy like yours, the battle of faith is daily. Believe Him for today, and ask Him for the faith to believe Him again tomorrow.

Ed

THE PAIN

How I made it through my most excruciating moments of suffering.

I remember how awkward I used to feel delivering sermons covering biblical passages about suffering. I would do my best to be true to the texts of Job, the writers of the Psalms, James, Paul, or the writer of Hebrews, but I intuitively knew that I could not fully appreciate their words. The disclaimer I always added to my exposition was "All my suffering has been self-induced, the consequence of either sin or bad choices. I would not presume to understand what these words must mean to those who truly suffer in ways we or they do not understand because it just seems so unfair, so unlike God to allow someone who deserves better to be in such agony."

That all changed the night this disease almost killed me. The sudden onset of this malevolent lymphoma, which oncologists report leads to more suicide than any other cancer because of the malaise, thrust me into Job's world. "Hand me a potsherd," I found myself saying, "so I can scrape this dead, flaky, heinously irritating skin from my body."

The two most challenging experiences facing those who must endure these unspeakable maladies are pain and misery. They are not the same, but each pushes the senses and psyche of humanity to their absolute limits. They are alike in presenting a need for momentary therapies that help the victim through literally one more second with a hope that must sustain for seconds ... then minutes, hours, days, and even months.

If I may, I want to offer my personal insights and the experiences that pulled me through and are pulling me through my battle with pain and misery. Since my worldview is Christian, the Bible's words and the Spirit's comfort are central to my coping mechanisms.

PAIN

Pain is the sharpened tip of the spear of whatever torments you and me. Whether an emotional throbbing of a broken heart or the physical ache of a shattered body, there are times when the hurt peaks with an acidic intensity that takes our breath away and demands the attention of every nerve ending and conscious thought. There is desperation. When you catch a glimpse of yourself in the mirror, you see wild eyes and a contorted face that used to be yours but now resembles some macabre caricature of who you once were.

My unique pain centers on the flaming, all-consuming irritation of my skin. When the leukemia erupted, one doctor explained, "Your blood is ticked off and it takes it out on the skin." I knew when I was rashing; I could feel it in the beat of my heart—the pounding of the blood in my carotid arteries and the whoosh of blood in my ears. Then the blood would boil from underneath my skin and turn it bright purplish red. The agony was excruciating.

First the heat, then the insane itching, finally the weakness as my body began shaking from the effects of exfoliating skin. As my skin fell to the ground in talcumlike cascades, and I lost the ability to regulate my temperature, some primal instinct shook my body uncontrollably, jerking my limbs and convulsing my muscles as if I had been stripped of my flesh and thrown on a snow bank.

This current episode has been more of a slow burn accompanied by the most insistent and distracting itch I have ever experienced. This drug reaction has turned my sweat caustic. As the moisture erupts from the folds of my skin, it sears every molecule of epidermis, leaving second-degree burns—only to smolder until the next round of sweat penetrates even deeper.

What the two experiences share is acute pain I never imagined existed, an evil hurt that focuses my every energy. During these times, I use what I can only call my "red-alert conversation with God" therapy.

Falling back on some of my favorite verses from the Scriptures, or the most comforting truths about the personal relationship with the Lord Jesus I entered into as a young man, I repeat the verse or the truth over and over again. I always begin with Philippians 4:13, a sentence from my Father's Word that has seen me through these despairing times:

> I can do all things through Christ who strengthens me. (Phil. 4:13)

Then I discipline my mind to say this over again and again with the emphasis on a different word each time.

"I can do all things through Christ who strengthens me."
"I can do all things through Christ who strengthens me."
"**I** can do all things through Christ who strengthens me."
"I **can** do all things through Christ who strengthens me."
"I can **do** all things through Christ who strengthens me."
"I can do **all** things through Christ who strengthens me."
"I can do **all things** through Christ who strengthens me."
"I can do all things **through Christ** who strengthens me."
"I can do all things through **Christ who** strengthens me."
"I can do all things through **Christ who strengthens** me."
"I can do all things through Christ who strengthens **me**."

Interspersed with these recitations is an ongoing conversation with the Lord Jesus, as if He is in the room with me, because His Word says that He is with us always, the ever-present Lord who comes near to the brokenhearted. The conversation goes like this:

Okay, Lord, You say I can do this. Show me how. I don't think I can, but You say I can. So right now, for one more minute, give me the ability to do this!

Here we go, Lord. Here it comes, and the pain is unbearable. I cannot do this, no way. Impossible. It is more than I can stand, but You say that I can do this through You. You told me You had strength to give me that will help me do this. Well, now is the time—give it to me now, right now. Not in five minutes, not in a few days. This is the time when I need this, and I am claiming this strength. If You say I can do all things, it surely includes this because this is something that I have to do. You have given me no choice, therefore, my sweet Lord Jesus, help me now. Me, the one You have promised this to.

I used this with a variety of verses that have guided me through these bouts with hurt. Some of the ones I quoted back to the Lord in this conversational style:

Restore me, Lord God of hosts; cause Your face to shine upon me and I shall be saved. (Ps. 80:3)

O Lord, You have pleaded the case for my soul. (Lam. 3:58)

Call on Me in the day of trouble; I will deliver you, and you shall glorify Me. (Ps. 50:15)

Sometimes I found more comfort in a particular truth from the Bible or theology. The Fatherhood of God, the Lord Jesus as the Good Shepherd, the Holy Spirit as Comforter, Jesus' promise that His sheep hear His voice, or the mercies of God toward those who suffer.

These conversations went something like this: The pain begins, the panic grabs my heart, and I would say,

O my Father, I need You now. I need You to be the Father You promised me You are. The One who sees me as Your special concern. The One who protects me, watches over me. Watch over me now, right now. This is my time of need, my Abba

Father. My Daddy who never fails, don't You see this? Of course You do. Come to me; help me. I cannot do this without You. You must be the Father I need. You say You count my tears in a bottle and that they are precious to You. Well, here come a few hundred more. See them, count them, consider them, and please do not disregard them. O my Father, I choose to trust You as the Father I need. Be more powerful than my pain, more tender than my hurt.

Son of God, Lord Jesus seated at the right hand of the Father, I appeal to You as the Lord who is high and lifted up, the dispenser of gifts and miracles to Your people. I need You; I need You now. You were so right to know that I would desperately need to know that You are the Good Shepherd, the One who never fails His people. You promised to care for me in such an intimate manner that I would hear Your voice. O, my Lord who suffered for my sin, the One who knows agony personally and experientially, the God who came down to experience every threshold of pain and suffering so that You are a High Priest who sympathizes with what I am feeling right now … O dear God, O Jesus my Lord, I need to hear Your voice. I need to know that You are here with me. Be near to me now in a way You have never been close to me before. If you have a still small voice, whisper in my ear … please.

I know that many of my more conservative friends may feel a little uncomfortable with these paragraphs, but I can tell you that this specific request opened an extremely personal dialogue with the Lord Jesus that I had never experienced in the decades I have walked with Him. And could it be that you have yet to know the desperation of heart and soul that erupts into such a prayer? It was Him, not me, who said this about prayer: "You have not because you ask not."

And then there were the nights I cried to the Holy Spirit in a personal way.

Holy Spirit, my Lord Jesus told me that You came to be my Comforter. This is the exact moment in my life that I need Your comfort more than any other split second before. So, Holy Spirit, comfort me; comfort me now. Show me what it means when the Word of God promises that You comfort His people. Please comfort me. I'm not telling You how to comfort me; I just need to know that You are here and that Your comfort, not my discipline or my imagination, is making a difference. Make it real. Make it obviously from You, and do it now.

The results of this prayer often brought verses to mind, a nurse into my hospital room, or a call or visit from a friend that was so timely I knew it was the Spirit's answer to my plea for His comfort.

Supplemental to this therapy were some simple and practical techniques that were necessary. Sometimes the pain was so intense I had to literally stuff my pillow or a towel in my mouth and bite down as I screamed the conversation with God. A pharmacist friend recommended using a simple mouthpiece available at any drugstore. Next time I think I'll take this advice, because there were times when I bit through my tongue or my cheek, and I'm sure that the grinding did my teeth harm.

There was also the part my bride played in these desperate episodes. Sometimes when I just ran out of energy, she would take on the role of my advocate. She, not me, would read the Scriptures and plead with God on my behalf as I sometimes faded in and out of consciousness. How wonderfully soothing to hear my life partner praying prayers of faith over me.

Finally, I or we would fall in a heap, exhausted. Our last minutes were literally spent on our knees next to our bed with our faces before the Lord, hand in hand. Our cry was simple *Please have mercy on us, Lord. Mercy, my Lord, mercy please. In Jesus' name, mercy please.*

Then we would fall asleep. Most of the time with quiet tears that graciously drew us to the peace of His arms, which would uphold us until the next time.

In closing, there is one very obvious point I have to make, my friend. This is not a "technique" to pull out of your spiritual hat in a moment of need. This is a therapy for those who walk with Him. It is only by abiding in His love and guidance as we walk by the still waters of everyday life and learn to trust Him for the minor emergencies and disappointments that we gain the strength of faith and comforting truths that will steel our soul in our personal day of our trouble.

So what would the Lord say about your life? I mean today, over the last few weeks, the last month, the two years that you just completed on this earth? Would He say that you are on a trajectory of drawing closer to Him and accessing the spiritual resources you have in Him? Or are you becoming more dependent upon your own strength and the circumstances of your life as your "coping" apparatus?

Are you the type of Christian who lives for the next fun event, such as a getaway or a remodel, as your source of fulfillment and meaning? Only you can answer that question. But that trip to Paris, that meteoric career, that bulging portfolio, or new kitchen will mean nothing when you face the inevitable emptiness of life on earth. Your heart will break on the shallowness of external happiness as you find your soul dry as dust and your heart unable to draw from the Living Water the Lord gave you freely when you believed in Him. Neglecting what you really needed from Him, you have gone to the well of your own self-sufficiency for so long that your spiritual muscles have atrophied.

What is one change you can make today that will turn your life hard toward God? Maybe you need to earnestly study God's Word, not as a student but as a practitioner. Some of you need to engage in the fellowship of a local assembly of believers. Others need to learn to walk with Him under the mentoring relationship of a more mature believer.

All of us would admit that we could entrust some corner of our life to Him in a more abandoned manner. The only way to face the crisis as a maturing disciple of Christ with categories in your mind and experiences in your heart that will glorify Him is to trust Him for what He is asking you to trust Him for *today*.

What is that? Do it, my friend. Do it now. You cannot get out of this life apart from these desperate days. This is a sin-stained planet full of pain and uncertainty. The only certainty for the child of God is His absolute ability to care for us as the Only One who is perfectly reliable and strong.

Your friend,
Ed

THE MISERY

How I deal with the misery of a chronic disease.

❧

The two most challenging experiences facing those who must endure chronic suffering are pain and misery. Since they are not the same, I have found that I need two different spiritual coping strategies.

MISERY

Misery involves pain, but it is more of a condition than a sensation. Misery is less demanding but more exhausting than pain, the undeniable evidence that your life today in no way resembles the life you knew before this tragedy, the growing and haunting awareness that your life may never be the same. Where pain is more of a snapshot of your affliction, misery is a short documentary covering your agony.

Whether the story is about your shatteringly unfamiliar emotional world brought on by whatever is breaking your heart, or your alien experiences of pills, waiting rooms, CT scans, prognoses, insurance claims, biopsies, and medical preoccupations your physical emergency has plunged you into, there are times when the contrast between *your past and formerly anticipated future* and the *actuality of your present condition* steals every bit of hopeful and positive energy from your soul. There is a new rhythm to your life you cannot deny when you take an honest look at what now defines your daily routine. You unexpectedly catch a glimpse of the "new you," which forces a more objective outlook, and you admit what others must be thinking. Because if *you* were watching you, you too would conclude that there is little hope for this miserable creature.

My unique "misery cinema" surrounded the battle to stabilize my temperature as the leukemia burned ever-deepening layers of skin from my bloated body. I would wrap myself in an old quilt most of the day—its bloodstained, body-fluid-discolored patches offering undeniable proof that life had changed. Inevitably, even the heavily padded and gratifying warmth of the quilt could not contain the heat streaming from my capillaries through the compromised skin. Shaking uncontrollably, I knew it was time to face the worst misery of my life, what I came to call my "greased pig" experience.

Keep in mind that my once-fit fifty-year-old body had morphed into a swollen, purplish red, moon-faced distortion of its former self. I hated seeing my new Jabba the Hutt figure in the mirror and the horror in friends' eyes when they saw the new me for the first time. Bloated and disfigured from the disease and the medications to inhibit its advance, I was, in a word, *gross*. The only cream capable of sealing my skin enough to retain heat was Eucerin, not the lotion but the cream. Did I say cream? It felt more like *paste,* and my only remembrance of the stuff was watching my girls use it to take off the ridiculous face paint they experimented with during their excessively made-up adolescent years.

I would steal away into my bedroom, a tub of lard preparing to apply a tub-o-lard to his body. One bath towel to sit on, another to protect the carpet from my gelatinous feet, and a fan I knew I would need sooner rather than later. Judy would come in, and we would begin spreading the salve, watching it literally melt into my superheated skin. For about five minutes, comforting warmth would return to my body—only to morph moments later into a suffocating coat of gel that caused sweat to pour. Then out came the fan, for about ten to twenty minutes of pure, unadulterated misery.

Early on in the experience, I called on every spiritual resource and procedure I knew of, but nothing worked. So I sat in front of the fan, weeping as the misery drained hope from my mind and, more dangerously, faith from my heart. The pain was intense, but the misery was more than I could bear on my own.

Then I received an e-mail from my friend and teacher Bruce Wilkinson, who had graciously taken me on as a mentor before he knew I would become such a basket case. Bruce's advice initially put me off, even angered me. His counsel? Praise God!

Praise God? I remember thinking as I abruptly closed his e-mail. *Praise God? Who are you, Bruce Wilkinson, mister Jabez with all your stardom, comfort, and blessing, to tell* me *to praise God when you have no idea how it feels to be me? When your world falls apart and your skin falls off and the doctors tell you that you have maybe months or at most a few years to live, then* you *praise God. I need help, and you just rubbed salt into my wounded heart in a way that could not be more real than if you rubbed rock salt into my tender skin!*

This was not the first time I had reacted against one of

Bruce's suggestions—only to later discover the wisdom of his recommendation. The Holy Spirit began to whisper reminders of Bruce's obvious personal commitment to me and past penetrations of the deceptions of my heart that for some reason only Bruce had seen. Begrudgingly opening his e-mail again, I read the entire message.

Bruce had presented four or five specific groupings of reasons to praise God. Some categories focused on my past experiences with the Lord Jesus, some on biblical and theological truths that had become precious to me in my walk with Him, and some looked to my future in Him, the confident expectations the Bible calls "hope."

As the Lord began turning my heart toward Bruce's words, in shaky handwriting I scrawled a verse, truth, remembrance, or expectation after each bullet point. This e-mail turned worksheet turned desperate need for deliverance from gloom became my twice- to thrice-a-day antidote to the hopelessness of my misery. Soon I memorized the entire half-hour process.

- Five truths about your relationship with God that have been most meaningful to you over the years.

- Four Scriptures or passages that remind you of Christ's love for you and give you confidence that you are His special concern.

- Six times in your past that you have seen His hand on your life in dramatic ways that you could not deny, times He has made clear to you that He is there and watching over you with loving care.

- Three reasons you are sure that no matter what happens to you, He is guiding you toward His loving purposes for your life.

The power of praise lifted my life beyond the misery. Transcending my earthly reality, it called my redeemed heart to all that is eternally true for the child of God. In ways I did not understand at the time but have come to appreciate, praise turned my woe to worship. Remarkably, I found myself actually looking forward to the "greased pig" chapters of my day.

My purpose here is more to recommend this discipline of praise to your miserable moments than to instruct you on the Bible's teachings on praise. A great resource Judy and I have embraced is the little book *31 Days of Praise* by Ruth Myers. Reminding believers that praise is the most basic act of worship, she provides clear biblical evidence of praise's power to strengthen your faith, help you tune in to God's enriching presence, activate God's power, cause profit that overwhelms your trials, cause you to experience Christ in your life, demonstrate God's reality in this wicked world, overcome Satan and his strategies, and bring glory and pleasure to God.

I'm sure all of this was happening as I sat before that fan with hands lifted high, verbalizing my appreciation of His goodness and His worthiness of my devotion and thanksgiving. As praise filled my heart—a heart that had been drained of all peace and joy—with a connection to the Lord I had never before known, I did not separate the blessing into theological or biblical categories. It just flooded in as a complete package of blessing and comfort.

Since my last knee replacement, Judy and I find ourselves once again "greasing up the old pig." Though my condition isn't as severely miserable as it was six years ago, the steroid cream that calms down this drug rash feels eerily similar to the pasty mess back then. When we spread it on, my pores feel dangerously clogged and the heat builds behind the congested mass. I throw the covers off the bed and turn the fan on my sweating body for relief. As desperation probes at the defenses of my soul, I always turn to an old recipe—the discipline of praise my friend Bruce taught me. Familiar sentences buried deep within my heart flow from lips that know the power of praise in a believer's life:

> *Father, when You saved me by grace (Eph. 2:8–9), You also told me that You saved me to accomplish specific works You prepared for me in eternity past (Eph. 2:10). I praise You that no matter what is going on in my body, I will not miss one of these works, no matter how small or great that work might be. There is no way I can be "cheated" by this disease. Praise You for Your precious promise to use my life in exactly the way You had in mind on the day You saved me.*
>
> *Lord Jesus, Your Word tells me that there is nothing I am experiencing here on earth that is not absolutely and intrinsically appreciated by You. Not because You look down on me with compassion, which You surely do. But more than this, because You stooped down to live life in the physical confines of the human body, the same human body I am trapped in,*

> *the very organs, systems, and vital life support that seem to be failing me now. Oh, how I praise You that I am talking to a High Priest who can sympathize with my weakness, because there is no feeling of fear, no threshold of pain, no weariness of body You have not personally experienced. Praise You that You have brought these scars and feelings of my human condition into heaven to Your seat at the right hand of the Father. Thank You that You whisper into His ear, "He is weak and afraid. This is hard for him. He does not know what to do, but he is turning to You for help. I am his Advocate; I died for him and love him so. When You answer his prayer, don't forget his weakness. He is indeed but dust."*

In closing, I feel the Lord would want me to remind you again of a critical question only you can answer. This is not a procedure on the desktop of your life, contained in a folder titled "What I May Need Someday If Life Really Gets Bad." This is a deliverance for those who *walk with Him*. You will not be able to live off the fumes of my praises. They were embedded in the depths of my life by years of dependence on His Spirit, growing knowledge of His Word, experiences with His power, and the relational comforts of my redeemed status as His cherished possession in a new redemptive community, the church.

So what would the Lord say about your life? I mean today, over the last few weeks, the last month, the two years you just completed on this earth? Have you been drawing deeply from the immeasurable spiritual resources your original faith in Christ made available to your everyday life? Does every year fill your life with more appreciation of His love, the wonder of His power, and the wisdom of His Word's guidance? Or are you becoming more distant from the supernatural edge of all that it means to be a new creation in Him?

Are you the type of Christian who calls on Him only when life takes you beyond your own strength? Have you allowed your life to revolve around your own power so that you could spend your days in the illusion of control that lulls too many Christians into a dull counterfeit of what eternal life really offers? "It's not what I thought it would be when I trusted in Him, but it's safe and predictable." Only you can answer that question. But your need for safety and your fear of surprises will rob your life of the astonishing interventions with which He wants to fill your days. Your heart will grieve over the loss when you stand before Him at the altar to discover all that could have been. Until that day, you will face the inevitable misery in your future with a tragic emptiness the Lord never wanted for you.

You can change all of that right now. You can tell Him that you want to begin living in a way that invites His goodness into your soul and maximizes your *right now* experience of eternal life. You will find that He will soon present real and undeniable answers to this prayer of commitment that offer options you may never have recognized before. Someone will offer you a book, or maybe you will hear a sermon concentrating on a life change you know the Spirit is directing at you. Maybe you've been wondering if some twinge of guilt or unexplainable preoccupation over a specific shortcoming or need in your life is from God. Count on it; it is.

We can't deny our need to more carefully attend to His will, more fully partake of His provision, or more keenly experience His presence. If you were to ask the Lord today, "How can I begin to live my life in a way that a discipline of praise would more naturally flow from my heart?" what do you think He would say? To what specific point of departure from His best for you would He draw your attention? Where in your spiritual life would He place your hand so that you could feel, as He does, the weakness of your redemptive pulse?

Don't ignore Him any longer, my friend. Turn to Him as you beg Him to empower you to follow through in the days to come. Ask Him to make your life one that will stand against the misery you cannot escape in this life with your personal, intimately revealed discipline of praise.

Praise will save you from the most miserable moments life can throw at you.

Praising Him for the blessings of life,
Ed

LORD, SPEAK TO ME!

How I learned to ask for guidance, even when some of my friends thought I was a little weird.

Six years ago, I knew that the Lord's guidance to me was that I should pray my heart (healing) while doing everything the doctors told me to do. This covers 99.9 percent of the decisions facing those who are suffering from chronic or debilitating illnesses. Still, there are times when the "art" of medicine puts the sufferer in an in-between decision.

I am facing one of those today. The dermatologist looked at the new rash, not as severe or as involved as the one before. He feels it is a reaction to the antibiotic I'm taking. When I protested that I have taken this med for years, he responded firmly that science proves that a drug allergy can still occur. Then, when the surgeon looked at my knee, he said that he feels better because the skin is closing up with no new open lesions. He added that it's a good thing I'm still on the antibiotic. Finally, my internist said that if it was his knee, he would go off the antibiotic, but it's my choice.

So what do I do? Flip a coin? Put out a fleece?

One of the thresholds my disease pushed me through was

my fear of being titled a "mystic." If that word makes you a little uncomfortable, I'll simply ask if you believe that God guides His people. We conservatives seem much more comfortable with logic than with seeking the Lord's specific will for our lives. But last time I checked, GOD DOES LEAD! He has a specific will for you and me. This does not mean we can always discern that will with the precision we desire, but it does mean there's nothing wrong with asking for guidance.

Do you see the difference between the two? What I'm going to do over the next few days is *ask* God for guidance, not *demand* His guidance. But I *am* going to ask!

Scripture is full of the Lord's very specific guidance to His people. He told Paul to quit praying about the thorn in his flesh and directed the apostles to specific cities in the New Testament world. Every great leader of the church shares in his or her biography of the times when they "just knew" the Lord wanted them to take one option over another.

So I ask.

I believe that my tender Shepherd wants to show me the way. I believe that the Spirit wants to comfort me. I believe that God guides.

Would you join Judy and me in this prayer?

Father, please give Ed clear guidance concerning the choice to continue with the antibiotic. In whatever way You can—peace of mind, still small voice, or just an understanding of what You want for him—let Ed know Your choice.

Call me a mystic; I prefer to view this as spiritual.

Facing the options with the Lord's help,
Ed

DADDY CRIES

How suffering taught me some difficult lessons on manhood and how my heart became more compassionate.

My daughter Celia was a sophomore in high school when I was first diagnosed with this ferocious leukemia and the accompanying malaise I never even imagined existed. Because my skin was falling off, leaving red sores behind that itched worse than the most severe case of poison oak I'd ever had, my wife, Judy, would have to rub heavy lotion into my skin about three times a day. The excruciating pain caused me to scream out with sounds I did not know were in me. I couldn't help it. This went on every night for months.

My days and nights were spent in the paranoid world known only by those who take heavy, heavy doses of steroids. With my emotions boiling just below my awareness, any disruption brought on rage. The daily routine, a severe depression, and the slightest reminder of what I might miss if I died (and many thought I would) ended in episodes of loud wailing. Many, many evenings I would finish these episodes by moaning feebly and pitifully to my God, "Mercy, Lord. Please, mercy."

I cried myself to sleep every night. And since I could not sleep because of all the medication and pain, every evening included at least three or four protracted cries.

One dark day, I was visiting my older daughter's home when a severe case of shingles erupted on top of my already sensitized membrane. The trauma was immediate and my reaction unmanageable. Even in front of my startled grandchildren I could not muster the self-discipline to muffle the screams and went to the bedroom to cry, shoving my face into a pillow to diminish the volume. I overheard Aimee saying to her younger sister, "Dad's pretty upset right now. Are you okay?" "I think so," Celia replied. "I've heard Daddy cry, moan, and scream a lot. I'm kind of getting used to it."

I hated that she had to learn about this side of life so soon, but I also knew that she was learning something about the manhood of her dad that we could discover no other way. Her ex-elite firefighter, ex-Army officer airborne soldier, stay-up-late-and-get-up-early, fitness fanatic, solve-everyone's-problems, always-strong-for-others dad was suddenly more human, more frail, and more needy than she or he had ever anticipated.

More than that, her self-assured father was becoming more like Christ than he had ever been. Real men cry, for themselves and others. The "realest" man who ever walked on earth was moved to tears many times.

The shortest sentence in the Bible makes this clear: "Jesus wept" (John 11:35).

Concise. Descriptive. Undeniable. No excuses. No need for explanation. Just the simple, manly truth about the Son of God.

Jesus wept.

I still cry myself to sleep sometimes when the reality of this disease hits me in a lonely or exhausted moment. Just this month, when my reaction to the drugs brought on symptoms so frighteningly similar to the leukemia they tell me lurks in my blood, the crying episodes spiked.

The blessing in all of this?

I cry about the pain and hurt of others too.

A lot.

Jesus wept because He is God and feels the pain of the world.

I cry because His gift of cancer gives me a glimpse into His heart.

> Blessed be the God and Father of our Lord Jesus Christ, the Father of mercies and God of all comfort, who comforts us in all our tribulation, that we may be able to comfort those who are in any trouble, with the comfort with which we ourselves are comforted by God. (2 Cor. 1:3–4)

Count on it, suffering friend. We cry with you for mercy as we claim this blessing for you.

Jesus Christ, not John Wayne, is the biblical model of manhood.

Jesus wept. So can we, and so should we.

Your crying friend,
Ed

SUICIDE

How to pray for the desperate sufferer.

There is a place where a mind overloaded by the desperate incoming signals of its traumatized body or mental anguish goes. This place seems to offer immediate release from the pain and misery the senses are screaming for. As the weariness sets in, this place can dominate the thought processes so that it appears to present the only option for relief. It is a place that only needs to make sense for a solitary, despondent instant. Though it is not the resting place a troubled soul desires, it is a final place its victims cannot come back from.

Suicide.

Unless you live in the world of professionals who deal with this issue—physicians and caregivers or counselors and therapists—the suicidal thoughts in the minds of most sufferers might surprise you. I know better now. This is why I always ask when I'm talking with those who hurt, "How is your secret thought life? Have you been privately considering the benefits of suicide?"

I remember the night I planned to end my life. With frightening logic, my thinking marched toward self-destruction with lockstep precision. *There is no cure for this. I can't stand another day of this.*

I've had fifty good years, a life full of love and meaning. I'm saved; I have no doubts about my eternal destiny. The moment I "fold my tent" here on earth, I will "pitch" it again in heaven to be with the Lord Jesus forever. This is too hard on Judy and the kids. I don't want to live like this. I have enough pills here to kill an army. I'll take two of these, three of these, a few of these. I need to take them right after Judy leaves for work tomorrow morning. I'll call this friend and ask him to come over. If he agrees to drop by at eleven, I'll make sure I'm dead by about ten-thirty so Judy won't have to be the one who finds me. There, all set. Let's do it!

I have no idea what or whom I meant by "let's." What I do know is that hopeless, chronic hurt and sorrow tempts even the strongest souls. Convinced that nothing could be worse than this, they long to move beyond the physical state to what they believe must be a better existence.

If you have yet to suffer beyond hope, you may find yourself protesting against this reality. "I would never try to kill myself," you say defiantly. "That's only for emotional or spiritual weaklings." You might be right. I hope you never have to face a night like I did when you surprise yourself by deliberating this most forlorn human decision. But what if you aren't as strong as you think? What if someone you love isn't as strong as you wish he or she would be?

What I'm saying, friends, is that suicidal thoughts are more common than you think. If you insist on viewing the world the way you want it to be rather than the way it is, that's your choice. But if you truly care about preparing for your own hopeless moments and the bleakest moods of those you love, you will read on.

First, an important disclaimer: Nothing I can offer will take the place of a good Christian counselor or psychiatrist. If you are contemplating suicide or if you suspect someone you love is suicidal, GET HELP NOW! My words come from zero—and I mean zero—understanding of the psychology of suicide. Trained and caring professionals, especially if their worldview is biblical, are the only ones qualified to determine if there is a dangerous leaning toward suicide and the best treatment toward emotional health.

I want to speak to the rest of us, those who know that we have no business playing psychologist with people's lives when so much is at risk. I believe Christians possess a spiritual asset that can make a difference beyond the reach of even the best secular psychologists and psychiatrists—prayer!

"Please let Ed live and serve" was the one-sentence prayer I asked everyone who cared for me to take before the throne of grace. Thousands from all over the world have joined Judy and me and the congregation of Church of the Open Door in begging the Father to let me live and serve in Jesus' name. From one-time acquaintances to lifelong friends, from everyday believers to some of the most notable saints of our age, this basic prayer has been and is being lifted to God in faith. With it, and as the Spirit has moved, individuals have added their own sentences, verses, and promises on my behalf.

I only have one explanation for my dramatic rescue from the edge of a self-planned trip to glory: God answered their prayers!

It was about two in the morning when one question came to me, three words that rescued me from the rim of a fatal decision and caused me to forsake the idea forever. Those three words?

What about Jackson?

Jackson is our first grandchild.

What about Jackson?

Whenever I thought about missing Jackson's life, I cried. This disease seemed ready to steal all that I had ever dreamed for the two of us in the five short years since his birth—Dodger games with all the Dodger-dogs, ice cream, peanuts, cotton candy, and souvenirs he wanted as I taught him the ins and outs of my favorite game, days at Disneyland when we would sneak away to be alone so that I could buy him stuff while none of the "posse of parents" was looking, and then there was the high country of the Eastern Sierras. Who was going to introduce him to my favorite place on earth?

What about Jackson?

What I most looked forward to was telling him all about the best life on earth—a life lived in abandoned trust of the Lord Jesus Christ, the life of a disciple, a follower of Christ.

What about Jackson?

As soon as those words came to my heart, a future dialogue came to my mind.

"Hey, Mom, who's holding me in this picture?"

"That's your papa, Jackson, my dad. He loved you so much and you two did everything together."

"Where is he now?"

"Oh, he's in heaven. He died when you were only five."

"How did he die?"

What about Jackson?

As smart and theologically astute as my daughter Aimee is, I knew immediately that there would be no words to offer to my grandson that wouldn't undermine everything I live for and all that I want for him.

What about Jackson?

On that night, I not only wanted the life of a disciple of Christ for Jackson more than life, I also wanted it more than death … even the death I so yearned for to stop the pain and misery.

What about Jackson?

I put the pills away right then and in one of the most decisive moments of my entire life I decided not to kill myself. Not that night or any night. And I have never thought of suicide since.

Do you want the Lord to whisper a rescuing thought to the heart of the one you fear may be losing the will to live?

Pray for that person.

Beg him or her to get help.

Don't try to analyze or persuade your friend; leave that job for professionals. You will probably say the exact wrong thing.

Pray.

Ask God to say the exact right thing. I believe that many times, He will. He did for me.

What about Jackson?

Jackson is eleven now. And his papa loves him, talks to him, and prays for him still. We have built memories of many Dodger games, countless trips to Disneyland, and I even taught him how to fish for golden trout … at ten thousand feet, in the Eastern Sierras.

That's because I'm still here, living and serving.

More convinced than ever of the power of prayer,

Ed

SNAKE OIL

Thoughts on those who offer surefire cures or hurtful advice. This section is intended for both the sufferer and the advice giver.

When the report of my health condition hits new hearts, especially Christian hearts, I'm always amazed at how little the response profile varies. There's a pattern I have come to expect when I ask for prayer or use my health to illustrate a spiritual truth. The size of the event or forum doesn't seem to matter. Whether sharing my story over coffee at a breakfast appointment, in a front-room Bible study, with my Bible class at a major Christian university, at large Christian conferences for men or families, at leadership retreats, or speaking in churches large and small, I can predict the main categories of advice, questions, and comments.

I always receive a lot of encouragement and comfort as people describe their own experience or a friend's encounter with cancer or suffering. Others promise that they will pray for me on a daily basis and even ask to be put on a prayer list. A few times one of the leaders present has halted the entire meeting or event so that he or she can lead the people in intercessory prayer for me.

But I have also encountered responses that are *not* so encouraging. The single most discouraging advice for most of us who are dealing with something chronic, deadly, or both is the "surefire remedy" that the medical establishment is "hiding from people." I must say that most of the time, these people are entirely sincere in their motives and understanding. What they do not consider, however, is how unkind all of this is to those who are suffering. To us, it is just one more offer of snake oil, the magic remedy only a few with insider knowledge are aware of, the cure for all your ills. As I've talked with fellow sufferers over the years, we all agree on four reasons why we wish people would not do this:

1. We simply do not believe that the medical community we interact with is withholding information that could help us. The doctors we have come to know care for us professionally and compassionately.

2. We have already studied every treatment option with our doctor's help and have seen how the science of medicine is superior to the undocumented reports of snake oil cures.

3. We feel awkward talking with strangers who are asking such personal questions about our treatment regimen, especially when these strangers come across as zealots for a certain alternative medicine.

4. We especially dislike it when we are offered "breakthrough" products that the recommender profits from.

With this in mind, may I offer some advice to those who find it so easy to speak authoritatively about someone else's life-and-death struggle?

- Don't come on strong.

- Don't argue with the sufferer.

- Accept a no graciously.

- Ask for permission to talk with them about a medicine or a product that *might* help them rather than telling them what they *must do*. If they say no, respect their decision.

- Don't make it cosmic. By that, I mean try not to talk about a global conspiracy to keep this great cure from the people who need it.

- If you will personally profit from selling this to them, offer it for free. And again, if they say no thank you, respect them.

I have helped many who are new to the role of official chronic sufferer with these one-liners:

- "This condition is an intensely personal matter, and I feel very comfortable with the therapy choices I have made."

- "My battle with this disease is a full-time job for me, and

I simply do not have the physical or emotional energy to consider new options."

- "If you don't mind, this is not the place to talk about this."

If they persist, here are some more:

- "You can appreciate why I don't want to answer such intimate questions to a complete stranger."

- "I think we're going to disagree about this, and that is fine with me. I hope you can see that this is the type of subject people will have strong and even conflicting opinions over."

And, if they refuse to take a no, you may need to pull out the heavy artillery:

- "I wish there was some way I could help you see how inappropriate it is for you to become so upset over my refusal to consider your recommendation when this is my life-and-death decision, not yours."

One of my most respected friends and Christian thinkers is Dave Burchett. Dave is a renowned sports director and a deeply devoted follower of Christ. When he and his bride, Joni, faced the trauma of watching the baby girl they had prayed for live her only year on earth in a tiny and irreparably flawed physical shell, he uttered one of the most insightful sentences, which has helped me accept some of the well-meaning but hurtful comments from Christian friends: "Christians tell me they don't know what to say, and then they open their mouths and prove it."

I think it would also help you if you knew the sentence I repeat to myself over and over when I am offering advice to those who are so overwhelmed by the circumstances of their lives that their patience is paper-thin:

"Hurting people are petty people."

By the way, I include myself in this category. My most petty and self-centered times have occurred during the weeks and months of intense suffering. If you don't believe me, ask my bride, Judy. I could give you about a thousand examples of my pettiness, but the morning I was rashed out and trying to find something to spread on my toast is representative of my pain-driven pettiness:

"Judy, are we out of jelly again?" I asked as I concentrated on my most important assignment of the day: Do not scratch!

"No, there is still a jar of strawberry jam in the fridge," she said. "Let me find it for you, honey." She reached back into the bowels of our refrigerator. "Here it is."

"I don't want *that* jelly!"

"What's wrong with *this* jelly?" she asked.

"It's the lousy generic store brand. How many times do I have to tell you that this stuff sucks. It's horrible. I'd rather spread spit on my toast than this counterfeit excuse for jelly. Why do you insist on buying this junk? The pennies you save are worthless when nobody will eat this gag-in-the-mouth stuff!"

And that was just the beginning of my fourteen-point sermon on the worldwide evil of cheap jelly and how I did not want this wickedness invading my home and how this must be some secret conspiracy that she had joined just to discourage me and ...

On that day the brand of jelly in our kitchen suddenly became more important than the war in Iraq, the millions dying without Christ and without hope, the needs of our children and grandchildren, or the ministry of Church of the Open Door. The pettiness of my confused mind made the choice of jelly an eternal and transcendent issue.

Just so you know, I'm not preaching *at you* but struggling *with you* in what most of us discover is our most difficult assignment from the Lord Jesus: *Love one another!*

Grace is an absolute must on both sides of the equation. Those of us who suffer need to pump grace into the atmosphere surrounding us by trying to look past the stumbling remarks of their lips to the caring heart that their words express. Those who are just trying to help need to pump grace into the atmosphere with an expectation that the very one they are trying to help might not respond in the way anticipated.

There is a paragraph from Paul's letter to the Galatians about helping a fellow Christian who has stepped on a landmine of sin, when God has called others to their side to help them pick up the pieces:

> Brethren, if a man is overtaken in any trespass, you who are spiritual restore such a one in a spirit of gentleness, considering yourself lest you also be tempted. Bear one

> another's burdens, and so fulfill the law of Christ. For if anyone thinks himself to be something, when he is nothing, he deceives himself. But let each one examine his own work, and then he will have rejoicing in himself alone, and not in another. For each one shall bear his own load. (Gal. 6:1–5)

Though this applies specifically to Christians who have fallen into sin, Paul's words offer sound advice to any believer trying to encourage those whose affliction is not spiritual, but physical or emotional. As I read this paragraph, a few guiding principles jump out of the text:

- *Restore* in a spirit of gentleness.
- *Restore* with the humility of a fellow follower of Christ on this sin-stained and hurtful planet.
- *Restore* by performing physical deeds of kindness that take some of the weight of this tragedy off their back as you shoulder part of the load.
- *Restore* after you have thoroughly examined your own motives, weaknesses, and absolute need for the strength only Christ can give you.
- *Restore* with the confidence that you are not trafficking in unlived truth but offering counsel that you know

you either have lived or would live when your dark days come.

Most important, resist the temptation to bail out of Christian fellowship because someone has hurt you. Intimate fellowship is messy, my friend. But the sustaining comfort and joy of Christian intimacy eclipses the hurt and disappointment we encounter along the way.

Clinging to my friends in spite of our messiness and thankful for all who are shouldering the load of this pain in spite of my pettiness,

Ed

SPIRITUAL PANTING

How to survive the moments when the pain causes you to lose touch with the world around you.

As I fought for my life, my most challenging moments were those when the physical weakness was so severe that I lost the ability to relate to the world outside of my private thoughts. Just lying there felt like a passive admission that I was losing the struggle against the evil trying to destroy my body. But when I tried to pray, I simply could not pull my reflections together enough to push connected sentences to God.

Somewhere in the murky yet desperate creativity that accompanies these most forlorn moments, I remembered an old technique I had learned in the early years of the Jesus Movement. Dr. Bill Bright authored a little booklet on the Spirit-filled life that taught us what he termed "spiritual breathing." Since it had a picture of a dove symbolizing the Holy Spirit on the front, we called it the birdie book and learned to "exhale" confession based on 1 John 1:9 and "inhale" the power of the Holy Spirit. As a young believer, "spiritual breathing" proved to be one of the most practical tools in my daily walk with the Lord Jesus. By now I've heard all the debate over the theological precision of Dr. Bright's tract, but I know that his words taught me to live with an expectation of power when my life was aligned with the will of the Spirit.

This personal experience with the powerful and practical simplicity of spiritual breathing generated a parallel technique I call "spiritual panting." During my more lucid times of strength, in the small gaps between the onset of acute weakness, I condensed the two deepest desires of my life into two words—*healing* and *revival.*

If my life were to count more for the Lord Jesus, He would simply have to heal me—at least to the degree that I could carry on in ministry. I decided to inhale a request for healing. If I had the energy to supplement that one-word prayer with a verse, I would pray my personal paraphrase of Psalm 80:3: "Restore me, Lord God of hosts; cause Your face to shine upon me and I shall be saved." Though the psalmist was requesting corporate deliverance for Israel in the context of the psalm, his words so perfectly expressed my longing for healing that I applied it to my solitary request. To ask the Lord God of hosts—the Master of the angelic host, both elect and fallen—to restore my frail body gave me such confidence in my Lord's ability to heal me. The picture of Jesus' loving face smiling down on me as I expressed my total reliance on Him brought a warm comfort to my heart.

If the Lord would grant me life and strength to serve Him, I had no doubt how I would want Him to use me. I want to live a revival with the leaders and people of this generation of Church of the Open Door. With the illustrious past of our historic church, we are surrounded by reminders of the glorious ministry of former generations. What must it have been like to be a part of those congregations who stood behind the amazing faith of Dr. R. A. Torrey, who built a four-thousand-seat auditorium when the congregation numbered less than one hundred! And then there were those stewards who responded to Dr. Louis Talbot's challenges and paid off the debt for that same building during the height of the Depression! Finally, consider the thousands of believers over the past three decades and around the globe who have been blessed by the radio teaching ministry of Dr. J. Vernon McGee that originated from the pulpit of Church of the Open Door!

God has used Church of the Open Door powerfully in the past. I could go on for pages and pages cataloguing the missionaries this church has sent and the ministries it has launched in partnership with the Bible Institute of Los Angeles (Biola University). I love pastoring a church with such a rich history and find it humbling to step into a pulpit formerly occupied by these giants of the faith.

Still, even the richest history is just that—history. All the spiritual fruit from those great years has already been picked. I have no illusions of leading like Torrey, pastoring like Talbot, or preaching like McGee. But there is something I can do—I can pray for revival. I'm tired of reading about revival, hearing about revival, and talking about revival. I want to live one. Right now, right here, on the hillside campus of this generation's version of Church of the Open Door.

So, I ask … again and again and again.

Father, please send revival to Church of the Open Door.

That is my exhale request. One word. *Revival.*

The undergirding verse is one of my favorites: 2 Corinthians 4:15. The New Living Translation states it this way: "All of this is for your benefit. And as God's grace reaches more and more people, there will be great thanksgiving, and God will receive more and more glory." The words from *The Message* stuck in my mind as I was "panting" this request to the Lord: "Every detail works to your advantage and to God's glory: more and more grace, more and more people, more and more praise!"

When Paul characterized his ministry to the Corinthians, his formula for success was simple: **More and more grace, more and more people, more and more praise!** I can't be like Torrey, Talbot, or McGee. What I can do is pump grace into the atmosphere of Church of the Open Door in every way I know how—in the way I treat people, in the way I lead the staff, in the way I preach the Word. Grace, grace, grace! I'm convinced that my part is to exalt His grace and ask Him for revival.

And so, from what they thought would be my deathbed six years ago, I panted this simple prayer, *Healing-Revival,* over and over again. I had to breathe or die—what a perfect opportunity to pray for the two deepest desires of my heart.

Healing-Revival.

Healing-Revival.

Healing-Revival.

It soon became a habit, a good habit. While I'm driving the freeways of Southern California, I have to breathe, *Healing-Revival.* As I fall asleep at night, *Healing-Revival.* When I wake up in the middle of the night, *Healing-Revival.* At the gym or on a hike in the high country, *Healing-Revival.* Just before I stand up to preach and the panic attack that admits the absurdity of me preaching in the pulpit of this historic church, *Healing-Revival.*

Friend, you have to breathe! Why not turn your inhaling and

exhaling into intimate conversations with your God about the dream He placed in your heart?

What is it for you? If I were to spend some time with you and we talked about your life, what would you say if I asked you, "If the Lord Jesus asked, 'What is it that you most want from Me so that you can serve Me in the way you most want to serve Me?'"

Why not say it now? Persistent prayer moves the heart of God.

That is why I ask over and over again, every day:

Father, please let me live and serve. Heal this failing body of mine so that I can serve You with all my might. And please, please, let me see revival at Church of the Open Door before You take me home to heaven.

May the Lord give you the faith to ask for your dream of eternal significance. I believe with all my heart that the beginning step in realizing that dream is to ask.

Healing-Revival!

In God's Grace,
Pastor Ed

QUESTIONS FOR PERSONAL REFLECTION OR GROUP DISCUSSION

Chapter 1

1. What circumstances in your own life have caused you to question God's goodness? Who did you have to support you and pray with you through those troubling times? Take some time right now to thank God for bringing this person into your life.

2. Pastor Ed found comfort in the story of Lazarus and his sisters. Are there any other passages that have brought you comfort over the years? Write them here or in another place where you can remember them. Again, take some time to thank God for speaking to you in this way.

3. How does it make you feel to know that you have an Advocate sitting at the right hand of the Father, reminding Him of the circumstances you're going through in this life? How might thinking of Jesus in this way change your approach to prayer? How might this affect your walk in general?

4. What does it mean to you to "live expectantly"? What might this look like in your own life today? How can you improve this area of your walk and your life?

5. How does it make you feel to think that there may be a special blessing reserved for you because of your suffering? How can you grab hold of this blessing, and keep hold of it as you move forward in life? Pray right now and thank God for this blessing.

Chapter 2

1. How would you describe your own prayer life? Are you a "reporter" or a "requester"? How do you feel about this in light of what Pastor Ed had to say on the subject?

2. What do you think kept Mary and Martha from sending for Jesus right away when their brother became sick? In what areas of your life do you feel like it's more important for you to "bear the burden" than it is to ask for help?

3. Is there anything hindering your prayer life right now? Keeping you from pouring out your heart to God? Fear? Apathy? Melancholy? What can you do to address these issues?

4. Pastor Ed's mentor Charlie White prayed a powerful prayer at his deathbed. What about this prayer resonated with you? Why?

5. Are you suffering unnecessarily right now? Missing out on the comfort God has for you? Take some time right now to pray and ask God to strengthen and comfort your life in these areas.

Chapter 3

1. Have you ever felt let down by a close friend? By Jesus? How did you work through that pain?

2. Have you ever been envious of the blessings you perceived others to receive in spite of your own? How did you deal with this? How could asking "why" help with this in the future?

3. Why do you think Jesus allowed Martha and Mary to despair for several days before He brought Lazarus back to life? Why didn't He tell them of His plans to glorify God through their tragedy?

4. If you were one of the disciples, what would you have thought of Jesus' decision to stay in Perea after He heard the news? Why do we sometimes not trust Jesus in the

here and now as much as we might have if we were with Him in Israel?

5. When we are in the midst of tragedy, it is sometimes difficult to look forward to what God has in store for us in the future—how He might use these circumstances for our good. Take some time now to ask God "how" He might be trying to use your personal tragedy for His glory. Ask Him to renew your confidence in His love.

CHAPTER 4

1. Have you ever been hurt by people who didn't know what to say, and then "opened their mouth and proved it"? How do you now view these people in light of what Pastor Ed has to say in this chapter?

2. Have you ever felt the Lord ask you to do something even though you didn't understand why or didn't know how? What were the circumstances? How did this request make you feel?

3. What do you think Jesus meant when He said, "If anyone walks in the day, he does not stumble, because he sees the light of this world"? How might your life look different if you always walked in the light of the day?

4. What does it feel like to know you can do nothing to help a certain situation—in your life or another's? How do you think Jesus would have us act during such times?

5. Do you know of anyone in your life right now who has a broken heart? Take some time now to pray for this person and ask God how you can meet that person's needs.

Chapter 5

1. What is the worst news you've ever received? How did you react? Why?

2. Do you ever doubt God's love for you? How do you deal with this doubt? How do you think Jesus would like us to deal with this doubt?

3. How might your prayer life change if you were completely honest with God about all the things that bother you? How can you improve this aspect of your prayer life?

4. Why is it sometimes hard to remember the reality of Jesus' promises in the midst of our own "earthbound hopelessness"?

5. In order to help Martha remember and realize the reality of God's promises to His people, Jesus raised Lazarus from the dead. What might it look like if Jesus were to raise a "Lazarus" from the dead in your own life? Take some time right now to ask Jesus to do just that.

CHAPTER 6

1. Do you still remember the moment of your salvation? What about this moment is meaningful for you even today? If you're not sure if you've ever had such a moment but would like to know more, seek out a friend you know is a Christian to discuss some of these things.

2. Were there any friends involved with your salvation experience? If so, what were their names? Take some time right now to thank God for these people. If you're still in touch, take some time to thank them personally as well.

3. What do you think of the idea that Jesus doesn't ask us to get started making a new and better life for ourselves, but rather that "He wants to give us a new life to start living"? How is this truth reflected in your life today?

What can you do to better reflect this truth in your daily life?

4. How does it make you feel to know that Jesus had you personally in mind when He died on the cross to pay for your sins?

5. Pastor Ed said, "To live with the hope of heaven is to live with a lot to be thankful for." What are you thankful for right now? When is the last time you thanked the Lord for His sure promise of heaven? Take some time right now to thank God for the many blessings in your life.

Chapter 7

1. Pastor Ed said, "When Jesus comforted His friends, He refused to agree to their demands. But He did react to their tears and respond to their trust." What do you think of this statement? How does this meet with your expectations of how Jesus should act during times of crisis?

2. What does it feel like to be pursued by Jesus? Why do you think He doesn't want to give up on us?

3. What are some ways you have tried to run from God in

your own life? Why do you think is it so hard to turn back to Him? How can you work on this in your daily walk?

4. When was the last time you actually told God, "I'm mad at You!" Why is it so difficult for us to be honest with God in this way? How do you think God reacts when He hears blunt honesty from us like this? How would Jesus react?

5. Pastor Ed said, "The most satisfying and sustaining marriages, friendships, partnerships, and families are those that honestly address their differences and in the process of working through the pain move to ever-deepening levels of closeness." How is this truth reflected in your own life? Which of the relationships in your life could stand to have a little more honesty these days? Take some time right now to ask God to help you be more honest in every area of your life.

CHAPTER 8

1. Jesus often acted counter to the prevailing culture of the day. Telling the people to roll the stone away from Lazarus's tomb is just one example of many. What are some ways you can better reflect this attitude of Jesus in your own life?

2. If Jesus were standing in front of you right now saying, "Serve Me today—in the midst of your troubles and heartache," how would you react? Where do you feel Jesus wants you to trust Him more so that you could serve Him better? How can you depend on Him more?

3. Pastor Ed speaks of his cancer diagnosis as a "gift." Why do you think that is? What kind of faith does a person need to have in order to make a statement like that? How can you embrace that same kind of faith?

4. What do you think of the promise, "If you believe, you will see the glory of God"? What are some practical ways that you can show God and others that you *do* believe? How can you strengthen that belief as you wait for Him to reveal His glory?

5. Finally, Pastor Ed says, "There is a difference between God saying yes to your prayer for your specific need and saying yes to your prayer to show you His glory." How does it make you feel to know that God might say no to your personal request? Take some time right now to pour your heart out to God in prayer on this issue. Never stop being honest with God about how you feel, but at the same time ask Him to show you His glory. Above all else, we hope you believe He will answer that request.